Student Housing Rights Guide

Martin Davis and Graham Robson

Published in 2002
by Shelter, 88 Old Street, London EC1V 9HU.
020 7505 2000
Registered company 1038133
Registered charity 263710

ISBN 1 903595 09-6

Design by Janine Roberts, Shelter
Editing and layout by Davies Communications
Printed by Russell Press
Distribution by Turnaround 020 8829 3000

*The case studies in this book are all based on actual events,
but names and places have been changed where necessary
to preserve confidentiality.*

*While every care has been taken to ensure that information in this
Guide is accurate, neither the authors nor Shelter can accept liability
for any omissions or any consequences arising from them.*

Authors

Martin Davis is Principal Lecturer at De Montfort University where he has taught housing law to housing professionals and law students for the past 20 years. Throughout his time at De Montfort he has maintained close links with both the Accommodation and Student Union Welfare Services. He is also the co-author of *Housing Law Cases and Materials,* published by the Oxford University Press.

Graham Robson is a solicitor and Chair of the Department of Professional Legal Studies at the University of Westminster, London. He was previously a solicitor at Tottenham Law Centre. He has taught housing law to housing professionals and on undergraduate and professional law courses at the University of Westminster for many years.

Acknowledgments

Special thanks are due to Peter Harvie for putting forward the original idea and proposal for this book.

Thanks are also owed to a number of people who have helped during the production of the book in providing information and checking sections of the text.

In particular we would like to thank Dave Warman, Student Accommodation Services Manager at Northumbria University and representative from the Association for Student Residential Accommodation (ASRA), who has supported this project from its inception, provided invaluable reader comments and co-ordinated input from other ASRA members: Angela Bogg, Bryan Carroll, Vivian Chestnutt, Alan Edwards, Hilary Simmons, Elaine Watkin and Ian Webster, who acted as readers, and Alison Clemett, Colin Bradley, Philip Duke, David Hill, Grant Jackson and Val Nicholls who helped by supplying case studies.

Thanks too to Alwyn Jones of the Law School at De Monfort University, Jenny Stuart, Student Housing Services Manager at the University of Westminster, David Roberts, Solicitor at Tyrer Roxburgh & Co and visiting lecturer at the University of Westminster and Melanie Rees, Head of Professional Practice at the Chartered Institute of Housing.

In addition, our thanks go to the following Shelter staff for their support and advice: Nick Beacock, Campaign for Bedsit Rights Manager, Steve Povey, Senior Solicitor Legal Services and Imogen Wilson, Head of Publishing.

Finally, we would like to thank all our students for all that they have taught us over the years.

Martin Davis
Graham Robson

Shelter

Shelter's vision is that everyone should be able to live in a decent and secure home that they can afford within a socially mixed neighbourhood where people feel safe, can work and fulfil their potential. Shelter is Britain's largest homelessness charity, with a network of over 50 housing aid centres and projects providing advocacy and advice at a local level for people in housing need. The start of Shelterline in 1998 marked the launch of Britain's first 24-hour free national housing advice line; the telephone number is 0808 800 4444. The start of Shelternet marked the launch of the UK's first website solely for people to get information about their housing problems; the address is www.shelternet.org.uk. Every year Shelter's services help well over 100,000 people.

For further information about Shelter, please contact:

Shelter, 88 Old Street, London, EC1V 9HU; Tel: 020 7505 2000; **www.shelter.org.uk**

ASRA, The Association for Student Residential Accommodation, promotes and supports the professional activities of staff working in all areas related to the provision and management of student accommodation in universities and colleges and other organisations with an interest in student housing in the UK and Ireland. The association provides information and advice through its website – **www.asra.ws** *– as well as newsletters, a mailbase, regional meetings, training events, and an annual conference and exhibition.*

For further information about ASRA, please contact:

Chris Coogan, ASRA Administrator, 1 Lane Green Avenue, Bilbrook, Wolverhampton, WV8 2JT; Tel: 01902 844448; Email: coogan_in_2000@yahoo.co.uk

Contents

Chapter 3: Problems with the landlord   31

Chapter 4: Paying for your accommodation   41

Chapter 5: Problems with your accommodation   63

Chapter 6: Problems with neighbours   81

Chapter 7: The university or college as landlord   97

Chapter 8: Leaving (or being forced to leave)   **115**

Chapter 9: Further advice and contacts   139

Appendices   147

Subjects covered in this chapter include...

Types of accommodation available

Where to find a place to live

How long should the letting period last?

Some basic questions to ask

Starting out at college or university is an exciting time. Unless you are staying at home, it will involve having to find somewhere to live. Where you live can have a big impact on how happy (and successful) you are going to be at college. Most educational establishments will provide, or at least help to arrange, accommodation for first year students. This will be either their own accommodation or they will have an arrangement with other landlords under which accommodation is provided in your first year. A rather smaller number of institutions will provide accommodation for the entire duration of your course and it is more likely that you will have to find your own accommodation in later years. In a few places you may even have to find your own place to live from the beginning.

Most people applying for places on undergraduate courses through the UCAS system are offered them conditionally on the outcome of their A2 exams. Some universities will also provisionally allocate accommodation to new students conditional on their A2 results. In many cases it will become clear exactly where you will be studying and living only after the results come out in the middle of August. The situation is usually clearer if you have a deferred place, for example, if you are returning from a gap year.

Most, but not necessarily all, universities and colleges, will send you accommodation information automatically when they offer you a place on a course. Be sure to read the information carefully and follow instructions about when to return application forms. Institutions vary in their policies and procedures, depending on the availability and type of accommodation available. What you have to do to obtain accommodation at your chosen university may be quite different to your friends at other places. The timescales and the type of accommodation you are offered may also vary considerably.

If you are not moving into university or college provided accommodation you need to leap into action well before the beginning of term to ensure that you end up with somewhere decent and affordable to live. Never accept accommodation without seeing it first. Some colleges organise briefing sessions for students to help them find accommodation, typically in early September. Your search for the right place could take a few days, depending on availability in your area. If you have not got friends or relatives to stay with, you should book temporary accommodation before arriving unless the college has already organised this as part of its 'find a home' sessions.

Types of accommodation available

College and university halls of residence

Hall residents almost invariably have their own room, usually with a washbasin, but may share cooking, bathroom and toilet facilities with other students. Most halls nowadays are self-catering, though some provide meals and other services such as cleaning and bed linen. Many are really collections of bedsits or small flats with communal facilities but no catering or services. Most halls are run by the college or university but some university accommodation is managed by private companies e.g. Jarvis plc manages over 3,600 rooms and is developing a further 3,000. This type of scheme is likely to become more common.

Private halls of residence

There is an increasing trend for new halls to be built and run by private companies such as Jarvis or Unite. They may appear to be college halls and may be on land owned by the college or university but they are owned and managed by private companies. There is accommodation like this at, among others, the universities of Plymouth, York, Reading, Manchester, Oxford Brookes and Luton. There are a variety of arrangements but typically the college will have entered into a formal arrangement with a private company under which rents and services are regulated by a long term agreement with the college. The college determines room allocations but the company manages and maintains the accommodation, and collects the rent.

College houses or flats

These differ from halls of residence in that you will be living in self-contained accommodation which you may be sharing with other students. You are more likely to be regarded as a tenant or joint tenant and thus have a higher degree of independence and control over your accommodation. You are also likely to have rather more responsibility for your living space. See chapter 7 for more information on the difference between halls of residence and college houses and flats.

Accommodation managed by the college

Some private landlords and housing associations lease property to colleges which then sub-lease them to students. The accommodation may be let directly to groups of students or to student families. These are often called 'head tenancy' properties.

Living in an owner's home

While you would expect to have your own or a shared room, you may be living with the resident family as a lodger. This may involve eating with them and sharing their facilities. This can work out well if you all get on together. Alternatively, the arrangement could involve having a relatively separate existence. You may feel uncomfortable sharing accommodation with an owner who has a different lifestyle to your own. This is the most insecure form of accommodation and you can be required to move out with as little as a week's notice. On the other hand, you can also leave at short notice, which could be useful if you were looking for accommodation elsewhere.

Self contained accommodation

This is where you have your own accommodation or only share it with people you are living with. The sleeping, eating, washing and toilet facilities are not shared with anyone else living outside your accommodation. You will be responsible for the gas and electricity bills.

Bedsits

Bedsits are single rooms, often found in large houses. They can be self-contained and frequently have their own cooking facilities but shared bathrooms and toilets.

Shared houses and flats

Where a group of students get together and jointly rent a place from (usually) a private landlord. Sharing with friends can be an attractive idea and is generally a cheaper proposition. The search for accommodation is also easier (and possibly safer) if you are looking with other people. However, sharing can also create problems and having a manageable number of occupiers is likely to help the situation.

Bedsits are overwhelmingly to be found in the private sector. Self-contained accommodation and shared houses and flats are mainly found in the private sector but may be available from your university or college or housing associations, or (less commonly) local authorities.

Finding a place to live: where to look

University and college accommodation services

The obvious place to start is the college or university housing or accommodation service (or its equivalent) which can give you free help and advice on finding a suitable place to live. They will usually provide regularly updated lists of available private rented housing. They will be able to indicate which private properties are accredited by the university or college or may only advertise accredited properties. To be accredited, the properties will have to conform to minimum standards concerning safety and amenities. The accreditation scheme may be run in conjunction with other universities or colleges in the area as well as the local authority. Not all universities or colleges have full accreditation schemes, but most will operate some safety checks, e.g. a requirement to produce an annual gas certificate. Some college accommodation services also have excellent web sites with lots of useful local information.

Accommodation agencies

Accommodation agencies and some estate agents help people find rented accommodation from private landlords. They do this in return for a fee. It is against the law for accommodation agencies to ask a prospective tenant to pay a fee for simply taking down your details or providing you with a list of properties available. You should not pay a fee for being introduced to a landlord but if you accept a tenancy, you may have to pay for the cost of an inventory of furnishings and for administration costs, including the preparation of the tenancy agreement and taking up of references. Check in advance what the charge will be.

Local newspapers

Some will have daily or weekly accommodation adverts.

The internet

There are many ways into finding rented accommodation on the internet. As with any transaction on the net involving money and people you don't know, you have to be careful.

Local adverts

You may see adverts in shop windows or on supermarket notice boards.

Notice boards

Students who are looking for sharers frequently put up cards on notice boards at the college accommodation or housing services and around college.

Word of mouth

If you know of departing students who have good accommodation, ask if you can contact their landlord for the following year before you leave.

Retainers

In some parts of the country, landlords will accept a retainer over the summer to hold accommodation for the beginning of the academic year. It is not common for London landlords to accept a summer retainer.

Period of letting agreement

The length of agreement you are offered may vary in different parts of the country. In some areas student lettings will last a full calendar year. Elsewhere, contracts may last for 40 or 46 weeks.

It may be possible to negotiate a shorter contract, but this will depend on supply and demand in the particular locality. If there is a surplus of accommodation landlords may be prepared to vary the usual terms, particularly just before the start of the academic year, in order to secure a letting.

Some basics points to watch out for

- Is the property accredited by the college or university?
- What are the terms of the tenancy agreement you are offered? (see chapter 2)
- What do you have to pay and when? (see chapter 4)
- What does this cover e.g. gas, electricity and water charges? (see chapter 4)
- Do you have to pay a deposit and on what basis? (see chapter 4)
- Do you have to pay rent in advance? (see chapter 4)
- Is the property damp? (see chapter 5)
- Does it suffer from condensation? (see chapter 5)
- Does it have adequate heating and cooking facilities? (see chapter 5)

- How secure is the property? (see chapter 5)
- How safe are the gas and electric appliances in the property? (see chapter 5)
- What facilities are shared and with whom?
- Is the neighbourhood a convenient and safe place to live?
- Is there an inventory or list which states the condition of the property and furniture when you move in? (see chapter 2)
- Is the property subject to a mortgage? If it is, you could end up being evicted if the landlord fails to keep up mortgage payments.
- Does the landlord have insurance to cover your possessions? This is unlikely and you should arrange your own insurance.
- Is the tenancy (or licence) offered to you for a fixed period of time, for example six or twelve months? Is this too long or too short? This could be a problem if you need to leave earlier (see chapters 2 and 8).

Subjects covered in this chapter include...

Is it a licence or a tenancy?

What if there is no written agreement?

Periodic and fixed term tenancies

Joint and sole tenancies

Agreements for different types of accommodation

So, you have found your dream flat or house (or at least one that is not a complete nightmare). What should you do now? The obvious thing is to sign up immediately for fear of losing it to someone else. The moral of this chapter is to take a little time – not least because once you have entered into a contract it may be difficult to walk away from it without losing your deposit or risking legal action. Try to read through any agreement you are asked to sign as carefully as possible. Ideally, get it checked over by someone with relevant legal knowledge and expertise. This service may be available through your college accommodation office or at the Students' Union (see also chapter 9).

This chapter aims to help you decide whether to sign or not, and to understand any agreement you read. The chapter covers the five main types of accommodation available for students to rent – there is no particular significance in the order:

(i) halls of residence;

(ii) other university owned or managed accommodation;

(iii) housing association and other Registered Social Landlord (RSL) accommodation;

(iv) council accommodation;

(v) private sector accommodation.

However, before this a number of general issues that may be important are considered.

Is it a licence or a tenancy?

You might think that everyone paying to live in a house or flat owned by someone else would have the same legal rights. If you did, you would be wrong. The identity of the person or organisation you rent from can have a crucial bearing on the rights you acquire. In addition, you may be offered a contract to sign, which states that it is a licence rather than a tenancy. If so, be very careful before you sign. At the very least, the fact that you have been offered something which, if legally valid, allows you significantly fewer rights should give you some cause for concern.

What is a licence?

Legally, a licence is a right to be somewhere, do something or engage in some activity. People tend to think (naturally enough) of the piece of paper which confers the legal right(s) as 'the licence' (as in a marriage licence or an entertainment licence), but what matters is the legal right(s) obtained. In relation to housing, a licence to occupy property is a right to do so. The right is important as it stops the occupier being a trespasser, but it confers less legal status than being a tenant.

Why does this matter?

It matters because a licence confers significantly fewer legal rights than any kind of tenancy. For example:

• A licensee (the occupant) does not have exclusive possession (the right to internally 'manage' the property and 'exclude' others) which means that a licence agreement (if valid) can restrict your lifestyle significantly more than a tenancy (see also chapter 3).

• A licensee has no legal security in the property and can be removed at any time by the landlord on the service of four weeks notice and (if necessary) the obtaining of a court order (although for 'fixed term' licences other issues arise, see below and see also chapter 8).

• A licensee does not have the automatic right to complain about the condition of the property conferred on tenants by section 11 of the Landlord and Tenant Act 1985.

So, how can you tell whether you are being asked to sign a licence or a tenancy?

The first thing to do is to read the agreement (the real moral of this chapter!). Agreements which attempt to create licences use words like licensor and licensee, rather than landlord and tenant. It is also very likely (if they have been carefully drafted) that they will deny that occupiers of the accommodation have any exclusive possession over any part of the property. It is also possible that there will be clauses which state that other (unspecified) people will have a right to share the property or even that the landlord will.

The important thing is not what the agreement *says* it is (although that is not completely irrelevant) but what it is *intended* to be in practice. In all the leading court cases on the 'tenancy/licence' distinction it has been consistently stated that the court should reject 'shams' and be concerned with the 'substance and reality' of the agreement.

What this means for most students occupying property owned by a private landlord is that even an agreement which claims to be a licence is likely to be viewed as a tenancy. In most cases it will be very unlikely that the landlord intends to share with you or impose other occupiers on you against your will. The reality is that you will have exclusive possession in practice.

The main exceptions are:

• Where the property owner provides meals and/or cleaning or other services so that you are, in effect, a lodger in their property.

• Where you live in a house or flat with other occupiers who are not joint tenants with you (see further discussion of this below) and tend to move around the property as people come and go to the extent that no room can be said to be exclusively yours.

(The second situation is legally difficult and you should always take advice on it.)

For the key cases on the above see *Street v. Mountford* 1985 and *A.G. Securities v. Vaughan/Antoniades v. Villiers* 1990. The Street case is the classic example of a landlord trying to claim that a tenant was a licensee merely because her agreement said so, even though she had exclusive possession of her bedsit. The court held that a tenancy existed in practice despite the wording of the agreement. The case of Antoniades further illustrates that flat-sharers who signed apparently independent licence agreements were actually joint tenants. Their agreements were interdependent because in reality they occupied the flat jointly to the exclusion of anyone else. In Vaughan, on the other hand, the four flat-sharers only had individual licences, principally because they moved around to the extent that no room could be said to be exclusively theirs.

Is the position any different for other 'landlords'?

This is a difficult question. In the case of a university running a hall of residence or a council running a hostel, licences are more likely to exist simply because the exceptions mentioned above are more likely to arise. It is common for people to have to move round a hostel at short notice as others move in. It is not uncommon for universities to provide lodger/'hotel' type services in halls of residence.

However, it may be that the 'rules' are a little different as well. In *Westminster City Council v. Clarke* 1992 the occupant of a council hostel for vulnerable homeless single men was said to be a licensee, not a tenant. This was partly because the occupants of the hostel did not have exclusive possession in fact (partly because of the supervisory presence of council staff, partly because of a clause in his agreement indicating he might have to be moved around the hostel as circumstances required). However, another factor was the enormous difficulties the council would face in managing such a hostel if the occupants were tenants.

What significance might this have for students? It would be unusual for students, even if occupants of council or registered social landlord properties, to be in hostels. Clarke does not suggest that council or RSL landlords have an absolute dispensation to create licences where private landlords do not. Perhaps the issue is most interesting in relation to halls of residence.

Universities might argue that traditional catered and closely supervised halls are a natural place for licences to exist. This seems broadly correct.

Even in other halls where no services are provided and there is little close supervision the university is in a distinct position. On the analogy of Clarke, its responsibilities to the wider community (or at least the wider student community) and the difficulties it might face if it could not 'discipline' students by moving them or removing them, should lead the courts to be more sympathetic to claims of licences. This is however much more uncertain. These issues are discussed further in chapter 7.

Am I legally bound by all terms in an agreement I sign?

It is wise to assume that the answer is 'yes'. As a general principle you are bound by what you sign even if you failed to read the agreement. However:

• Some terms may be 'unfair' and so unenforceable in relation to the Unfair Terms in Consumer Contracts Regulations 1999. These regulations also apply to licences and tenancies. The regulations are discussed further in chapter 7.

- Some terms may be invalid in law. For example, if a landlord seeks to transfer responsibility for keeping a property in repair (see chapter 5) to her/his tenants this has no legal effect.

- Some terms may be inconsistent with other occupiers' rights guaranteed by law. For example, if a tenancy agreement attempts to give a landlord unrestricted access to the property at all times this seems to be inconsistent with the tenant's right to 'quiet enjoyment' (see chapter 3). A term which prohibits an occupant from having guests staying with them in the property seems to be inconsistent with a tenant's (although not a licensee's) right of exclusive possession.

- Some terms may be unenforceable because their effect has been misrepresented earlier by the landlord or the landlord's agent.

If you feel that a term you are concerned about falls into any of the above categories, it is wise to seek legal advice before signing the contract.

Can I cancel an agreement I have entered into?

Generally, the answer is 'no'. You are bound by agreements you have signed or otherwise entered into unless you have been the victim of fraud, misrepresentation or undue influence (the latter are matters of general contract law which are beyond the scope of this book).

However, if you enter into the agreement electronically, over the telephone, or via some other form of 'distance communication' (see below) the situation might be different. It may be that in such cases the Consumer Protection (Distance Selling) Regulations 2000 apply – and you have a right to cancel the agreement within seven days of entering into it.

The principal 'distance communication' circumstances listed in the regulations (Schedule 1) are:

- mail order

- letter

- telephone

- radio

- electronic mail

- fax.

The Distance Selling Regulations are not entirely clear as to which contracts they apply to, and conflicting views have been expressed as to whether they apply to tenancy agreements. However, the Office of Fair Trading seems to think that they do apply. If you think that they may apply to your situation and you are within the seven day cancellation period, take legal advice immediately.

Does it matter if I am under 18?

If you are under 18 when you make an agreement to rent accommodation the law is rather different – and not particularly satisfactory. You can enter into a valid contract because even though you are under age the law regards contracts for necessities like food and shelter as ones you can legally enter into. However, if under 18 a person cannot hold what is termed a 'legal estate' and given that a tenancy is a form of legal estate a person under 18 cannot hold a tenancy.

However:

• Recent case law suggests that an attempt to create a tenancy with someone under 18 results in a contract to 'convey' the 'legal estate' once they reach 18.

• A licence is not a 'legal estate' and so a person under 18 can validly hold a licence to occupy property.

• Another approach is to grant a tenancy to another person to hold on behalf of the under 18 year old until they reach 18.

Always take advice if you are under 18.

Periodic and fixed term tenancies

A periodic tenancy in law is one which needs to be continually renewed. So a weekly or a monthly tenancy needs to be renewed every week or month. However, there is no need to do this formally as every time the rent is paid and/or you remain in the property this is viewed as 'renewing' the tenancy.

A fixed term tenancy is one which is 'fixed' for a specified period of time, for example an academic term, six months or the academic year.

What are the main differences between periodic and fixed term tenancies?

• You can end a periodic tenancy by serving a valid notice to quit on your landlord. This has to be a minimum four weeks' notice even if it is a weekly tenancy (see also chapter 8). A landlord's position concerning termination of periodic tenancies depends on the type of tenancy involved (again see chapter 8). A fixed term tenancy cannot be brought to an end before the expiry of its normal term by the service of a notice to quit but only by the exercise of a 'break clause' in the agreement (if there is one).

• You will normally be bound by a fixed term tenancy for the period specified in the agreement. This means that if you leave before the end of this period you will be liable for unpaid rent. Most tenancies or licences that you encounter today are likely to be fixed term ones.

Landlords see fixed term agreements as providing them with greater financial security, in that the rent of the property is guaranteed for the period specified. It is unlikely that there will be a 'get out' ('break') clause in the agreement allowing you to leave (although fixed term hall of residence agreements often make exceptions covering illness or other emergencies). Many students wrongly believe that they have a right to leave accommodation they occupy under a fixed term agreement for personal reasons, most typically because they do not get on with other residents. This is not true – the circumstances in which you can leave (assuming there is no 'break' clause in the agreement) are very limited, being largely confined to the unfitness of the property (for further information see chapter 5). In theory a landlord has to make reasonable efforts to find a substitute tenant if you do leave and they cannot unreasonably refuse to relet to someone else. However, it would be wise not to expect too much, given how flat the student housing market may be in the middle of an academic year.

If you do enter into a fixed term agreement and later regret it, try to negotiate matters with your landlord. They may be willing to compromise, although in strict law they can look to you for your rent until a substitute acceptable to them is found (by you or them). For more information on rent generally, see chapter 4.

Joint and sole tenancies

A joint tenancy occurs wherever more than one person in a property shares a tenancy. In legal parlance joint tenants do not possess separate parts of the property, they are all equally entitled to joint exclusive possession of the whole of it. Joint tenants collectively possess one tenancy.

Sole tenants, even if they live under the same roof as others, only have a right to exclusive possession of any accommodation they separately occupy (typically their bedroom) although there may be joint use of other rooms such as kitchens and bathrooms.

How do you distinguish between a 'joint' and a 'sole' tenancy?

This is a notoriously difficult question. As always there are obvious cases: at one extreme the 'bedsit' occupier, even if a tenant, is obviously a sole tenant. At the other extreme, a group of friends approach a landlord's agent together, and sign one tenancy agreement containing all their names, following which they continue to occupy the property together and pay one rent for the whole. This is clearly a joint tenancy. However, other cases will be more uncertain, particularly where a number of occupiers live under the same roof and share some expenses in practice but pay separate rents to their landlord (not uncommon in student tenancies). An already complicated question is often made even more difficult by confusion with the linked but distinct question as to whether the occupiers share a 'single household' and so do not occupy a 'house in multiple occupation' (see chapter 5).

Indeed there is no single or simple test to decide whether a tenancy is sole or joint, but pointers include:

• Whether the tenancy contract is in joint names or (alternatively) there are several individual contracts.

• How the rent is paid, jointly or individually, and whether the property is stated to be let for one overall rent or a number of individual rents.

• Whether the tenants first approached the landlord or their agent as a couple/group or separately.

• Whether the tenants share – in any sense – a 'single household'. Although this is not crucial in isolation, as stated above, it may be a relevant factor in some cases. A 'single household' is one where the occupiers look after the property together and share expenses.

The distinction is important because sole tenants are only liable for their own rent and have only very limited liability for what other tenants do. Conversely, joint tenants are jointly responsible so that rent is owed collectively and there is equivalent liability for breakages and disrepair. So, if a joint tenant 'walks away' from a fixed term tenancy (above), instead of regarding them as responsible for unpaid rent, the landlord can look to the remaining joint tenants to make up the difference. If an agreement, tenancy or licence, seeks to make sole occupiers jointly liable for matters like breakages this is, arguably, an unfair contract term and unenforceable (this is discussed in detail in chapter 7).

On the other hand, being a joint tenant does confer joint rights over the whole property occupied. A joint tenancy is one entire tenancy, not a number of interlinked ones. So if, for example, one joint tenant leaves, although the others remain liable for their rent they probably have the right to allow others into the property as their 'guests' (licensees) to, perhaps, help offset the cost.

Case

Five female students shared a house as joint tenants. One of the group, Rachel, sought advice when she wished to leave to live with her boyfriend. She had found a replacement male student but the others had objected and she felt they were being unreasonable, and, following disagreements within the group, unnecessarily spiteful. She was advised about joint liability, but that the group as a whole had to be realistic. She was advised to try and persuade the others to accept her nominated replacement if there was no valid reason to reject him, which there did not seem to be: he was in the same year at the same university, had a genuine reason for needing accommodation mid-year, and was willing to pay the final term's rent immediately. But the others still refused to accept him, and they did nothing to advertise the potentially vacant room or show it to prospective tenants.

Rachel went back to the Accommodation Office as relations within the house were strained. The joint liability was again emphasised, but she was advised that if she did decide to move out she should explain the whole situation to the landlord and inform him with whom she had left her key – or hand it to him. She moved out, and the landlord threatened to take the remaining students to court for the unpaid balance of Rachel's rent, which they eventually paid between them.

Comment

The landlord could have held all the tenants liable for the rent, including Rachel, but in a situation like this it is important to keep the landlord informed. The landlord may choose to ask any one of them for unpaid rent before any other. Similarly, a tenant who has simply not paid while living in the property may be sued for his or her share of the rent, but the others in the group are equally liable in law for the debt.

Halls of residence

If you are a first year student at university there has traditionally been a strong possibility that your first 'independent' accommodation will be in a hall run by your university. (In the case of 'old' universities there may be enough hall accommodation for other students as well, but this is less likely with 'new' universities.) In the excitement of being away from home for the first time, reading carefully through your hall agreement may be low on your list of priorities but you should make the time to do so. Some universities still present new students, on arrival, with their agreements for signature, giving little opportunity to read them through, let alone have them independently checked. This is, in our view, a bad practice – not only because it does not give an incoming student a reasonable opportunity to grasp what it is they are letting themselves in for, but also because it may have negative longer term implications for the university. It makes sense to ensure that students know in advance what their rights and responsibilities are and, in any event, a term which is seen to be imposed without opportunity for proper reflection is more likely to be 'unfair' in relation to the Unfair Terms in Consumer Contracts Regulations 1999 (see chapter 7). We would strongly advise universities to send out their hall agreements for students to check before they arrive at university. Where this is not possible, for example because a student has received a late offer or is travelling from overseas, students should be given time to reflect on the agreement and seek advice on it before committing themselves to it.

If you do get a chance to look over your hall agreement, it is reasonably likely (although not inevitable) that it will be stated to be a licence rather than a tenancy. It is explained earlier in this chapter, and again in chapter 7, that whether something is a licence or a tenancy is a matter of law and does not solely depend on what it says in the agreement. Our overall conclusion is that traditional catered halls are a very natural place to find licences rather than tenancies, whereas in halls which are more like collections of flats, the issue is much more debatable.

Given the advantages of living in hall early in your time at university it is doubtful whether the fact that the agreement you are asked to sign is a licence should deter you. A licence does give you less legal protection and less independent control over the property you occupy but in some cases it may be a licence in name only, and even where it is a licence in reality it will only rarely cause you real problems. As you will see from chapter 7, even if a tenancy, it is a 'common law' (non assured) one because you rent from your university or college.

It is more important that you read the agreement carefully (whether it is stated to be a tenancy or a licence) to check what your rights and responsibilities are. In particular, look for the circumstances in which you can leave the hall and terminate the agreement (these are likely to be limited), penalties for 'misbehaviour' and what the implications are of falling behind on your rent/licence fee (for example, potential withholding of your exam results or final qualification as well as eviction). See chapter 7 for more detail on these points.

Other university owned and managed accommodation

It is always important to know who your landlord is, partly for the obvious reasons of knowing who (ultimately) is legally responsible for the property but also because this may affect your legal status and consequent rights. In some cases you may find that your landlord is not who or what you expected. Increasingly, private landlords are moving into the student market to run 'managed' accommodation which has all the appearance of being a university operated hall. The accommodation may even be marketed through the college or university's accommodation service, almost as if it were university accommodation.

In other cases you may find that although the flat or house you occupy is privately owned, your immediate landlord is your university (which has let the property from the landlord, and sub-let it to you). These arrangements, often referred to as 'head tenancy' agreements (see chapter 7), have often proved attractive both to the property owner (who is secure in the knowledge that the day to day responsibility for the property is out of their hands) and to the university (which by such arrangements adds a significant number of new properties which can be directly offered to students through the university accommodation service).

As the university is your landlord, that is where you should turn with any problems of disrepair or defects in the property. Also check the extent to which your occupation (as it would be in a hall of residence) is interlinked with the university's disciplinary code (again, see chapter 7). Issues as to whether you are a sole or joint tenant may also arise (see above). Finally, because the university is your landlord, your tenancy is a common law (non assured) one (chapter 7).

Council tenancies

It is relatively unusual for local authorities to allocate tenancies to students. Council accommodation is in short supply in many areas, and students generally do not have any priority in relation to such a scarce resource. However, from time to time universities make arrangements with local councils for students to fill unpopular or 'hard to let' accommodation or to become interim tenants of property which is being redeveloped. Equally, you may be a mature student who already has a council tenancy prior to going to university. These two different situations may produce very different legal results.

If your council tenancy is granted for the purpose of enabling you to attend your course and the council notifies you in writing prior to the grant of the tenancy that this exception applies then you will not become a secure tenant (Schedule 1, paragraph 10, the Housing Act 1985). Instead you will only have a non-secure tenancy with limited legal protection (for more information about 'exempt' university tenancies see also chapters 7 and 8). Your tenancy will become secure in the somewhat unlikely event that the council subsequently notifies you that your tenancy should be regarded as secure.

If you are an existing council tenant the likelihood is that you do have a secure tenancy. If so, as the title indicates, you have a high degree of legal and practical security in the property. Sections 83 and 84 of the Housing Act 1985 provide that you can only be evicted on specified grounds and even then, in most cases, only if a court feels it is 'reasonable' to grant possession against you or in a few cases if you are offered suitable alternative accommodation (see chapter 8).

Detailed consideration of secure tenancies is beyond the scope of this book, and you may need to consult a more general book on housing law as well if you have a particular problem (for examples of useful texts, see chapter 9). However, the following points are worth noting:

- If your university is in another location and the time you spend in your council accommodation is limited, you need to be aware that to retain all your rights you need to continue to occupy that accommodation as your 'only or principal home' (s.81 the Housing Act 1985). This does not necessarily mean that you have to spend the majority of your time in it but you do need to keep it as your base.

- Although as a secure tenant you are entitled to take in guests/lodgers (s.93 (1)(a) the Housing Act 1985), you need 'consent' from your council landlord before sub-letting any part of the property. This consent should not be 'unreasonably withheld' (s.93(1)(b) and s.94(2) the Housing Act 1985). If you sublet the whole property your tenancy automatically ceases to be secure (s.93(2), the Housing Act 1985).

- You may not have a secure tenancy if your local authority has an introductory tenancy scheme and you have been let the property in the last year (the Housing Act 1996, Part V Chapter 1). See chapter 8 for more details on this.

All the above areas can be legally complex and you should seek further advice if they seem likely to affect you.

Housing association and other registered social landlord tenancies

The title of this section is complex. This is because Section 1 of the Housing Act 1996 created the concept of the 'Registered Social Landlord'. To be eligible to be 'registered' an organisation had, among other things, to be non profit making (see s.2 for the eligibility criteria). Most RSLs are housing associations and if you do have an RSL landlord it is far more likely to be a housing association than anything else. (Housing associations are a diverse group of non profit making, often charitable, organisations which provide social accommodation.) Nevertheless, the more technically correct general term today is Registered Social Landlord. In some parts of the country, it is uncommon for housing associations to let directly to students, and more common to find 'head tenancy' and similar arrangements instead. However, elsewhere housing associations play a significant role in the student housing market.

If, as is overwhelmingly likely to be the case, you entered into your housing association tenancy on or after 15th January 1989 you will have either an assured or an assured shorthold tenancy; whereas if you entered into a tenancy agreement prior to 15th January 1989 you are most likely to have a secure tenancy. (See the section above under the heading 'Council tenancies' for information about secure tenancies.)

If you entered into a tenancy agreement with a housing association before 28th February 1997, it will be an assured tenancy unless the association took steps to 'set up' an assured shorthold. Broadly this means that it created:

- a fixed term tenancy for at least six months

- where prior to the tenancy you were given a notice from the association stating that what was being created was an assured shorthold and which was in the form laid down by the Assured Tenancies (etc) (Forms) (Regulations 1988) or was 'substantially to the same effect'.

If your tenancy began on or after 28th February 1997 then it will be an assured shorthold unless an assured tenancy was specifically created (see the Housing Act 1996 s.96 and Schedule 7). You will need to look at your agreement carefully before signing it to see if this is the case. If you are in doubt, the housing association would probably be happy to discuss it with you.

If you do have an assured tenancy then you have a reasonably high degree of security in the property. As with local authority secure tenancies, you can only be evicted on specified grounds (sections 5 and 7 of the Housing Act 1988) although these grounds are somewhat more extensive than in the case of secure tenancies. This is discussed in more detail in chapter 8. In clear contrast to secure tenancies, however, you do not have a clear statutory right to take in lodgers, and there is no corresponding (even limited) right to sub-let. If that might be an issue for you, check what the offered tenancy agreement has to say. If it expressly prohibits sub-letting, then you will be in breach of your tenancy and so vulnerable to eviction if you do sublet (see also chapter 8). If it expressly allows sub-letting then, obviously, there is no problem. If it is silent on the matter, then s.15(1)(b) of the Housing Act 1988 implies into the agreement a term that sub-letting is not allowed without the consent of the landlord. Therefore if the question of sub-letting even part of the property becomes an issue, you should discuss it with the housing association.

As regards having lodgers, if the agreement allows this, then, of course, there is no problem. If it is silent, then you are probably safe to go ahead, in that your inherent right to exclusive possession as a tenant suggests that you have a right to have guests (even paying guests) living with you. If the agreement prohibits having lodgers, the law is somewhat uncertain, in that there seems to be a conflict between your inherent rights as a tenant and the express terms of the tenancy agreement. You will need to take legal advice on this. What is clear is that a term in the agreement prohibiting sub-letting is not breached if you merely take in lodgers. Effectively, a lodger is a licensee and a person living with you in the property should be seen as a lodger and not a sub-tenant if they share with you and lack exclusive possession of their own.

See the following section for details about assured shorthold tenancies.

Private sector tenancies

It is likely that, at some point in your time at college or university, and perhaps for the whole of your course, you will rent from a private landlord. In this context a 'private landlord' is any landlord other than your college or university, the council, or a registered social landlord. Until recently, most private landlords were individuals or small private companies renting only a handful of properties. Today, there are a number of large public companies moving into the student housing market. As some of these work closely with universities, and others provide 'hall type' accommodation, it is increasingly important that you check out very carefully who your landlord is. (Another reason for checking carefully is that your university or college accommodation service may have a list of 'approved' or 'accredited' landlords. If your landlord is on this list it gives you some degree of reassurance that the property has been checked over to see it is in a decent state of repair and that the landlord is more likely to behave responsibly.)

In the unlikely event that you have had your tenancy since before 15th January 1989 (or have taken over such a tenancy on the previous tenant's death) your status will be a Rent Act protected or statutory tenant. This gives you significantly enhanced rights over other private sector tenants both as regards your security in the property and even challenging the contractually agreed rent. However, as this will affect very few students it is not discussed further here. If you think you may have a Rent Act tenancy, consult another general book on housing law (for examples of useful texts, see chapter 9) and take legal advice.

If you took over the tenancy between 15th January 1989 and 27th February 1997, the law is as follows:

- If you went into possession without a written agreement or without an assured shorthold notice (below) or without having entered into a fixed term agreement of at least six months duration then you will have an assured tenancy (see above in relation to housing associations).

- To be legally valid an assured shorthold (AST) notice must have been in writing, correctly dated and given to you prior to entering into the tenancy. It should have been made clear that what you were entering into was an assured shorthold tenancy (see s.20, the Housing Act 1988).

If you took over the tenancy at any time from 28th February 1997 onwards, you can generally assume that you have an assured shorthold tenancy (the only real exception is in the rather unlikely event that an assured tenancy was specifically created). It does not matter whether your tenancy is periodic or fixed term. It does not even matter whether it is verbal or written.

What is an assured shorthold tenancy?

Before 28th February 1997 it meant a short fixed term private sector tenancy, where your only real 'assurance' as a tenant was a minimum six months security in the property. Since then, it means virtually all private sector tenancies, save for a few exceptional cases. If you do have an assured shorthold tenancy then (whether pre or post 28th February 1997) you are guaranteed six months in the property. If you do have a fixed term agreement for longer than six months, but there seems to be a clause in the agreement allowing your landlord to bring the tenancy to an end earlier, you should take legal advice. (See chapter 8 for further information.) You have no long term security in the property, although in practice your landlord may allow you to remain in the property after the original term has expired, or even renew the tenancy. In the case of post 28th February 1997 tenancies, assuming you do not already have a written agreement setting these matters out, you are also entitled to a written statement of basic tenancy terms from your landlord, covering

- the amount of rent payable and when it should be paid

- any arrangements for increasing the rent

- the date your tenancy began and the length of any fixed term.

It is illegal for your landlord not to provide you with such a statement within 28 days of receiving your request in writing (s.20A of the Housing Act 1988 as amended).

Are there any exceptions?

On the positive side it is possible (although unlikely post 28th February 1997) that you have an assured tenancy. This is discussed above. On the negative side there are some situations where you will not even have the limited rights guaranteed by possessing an assured shorthold tenancy, for example:

- You may only have a licence and not a tenancy at all. However, as already discussed, there are very few situations where private landlords can validly create licences rather than tenancies.

- You may not occupy a 'separate dwelling' and so fail to satisfy the condition laid down in s.1, the Housing Act 1988 for having any kind of assured tenancy (even an assured shorthold). This is only likely to apply if you have no separate accommodation at all (recent case law, *Uratemp Ventures Ltd v. Collins* 2001, indicates that something can be a 'dwelling' even if it lacks cooking facilities). You can have a 'separate dwelling' even if you share accommodation with others, so long as there is something which is 'exclusively' yours (s.3, the Housing Act 1988).

- You may not occupy the property as your 'only or principal home' (s.1(1)(b), the Housing Act 1988) and so, again, fail the basic 'assured tenancy' test. This is discussed above, in relation to council tenancies.

- You may have a resident landlord. At the very least, if you do, your tenancy cannot be an assured or assured shorthold. A resident landlord is one who resides in some other part of the building in which you live, even if there is no sharing with them, or even real contact with them (see Schedule 1 paragraph 10, the Housing Act 1988). In some cases you may 'share' with your landlord, or with a member of the landlord's family. Sharing includes the sharing of bathrooms, kitchens and even toilets. If you do share with your landlord, your legal rights are reduced still further.

In the above cases, you will be a non assured (sometimes called a Common Law) tenant (or a licensee), with no legal security at all, except for the fact that you must generally be given a minimum of four weeks notice to quit the property and a court order is required before you can be evicted (see the Protection from Eviction Act 1977, sections 3 and 5). However, if you share with your landlord, or a member of their family, then even this limited protection does not apply, although even at common law you will need to be served with a notice to quit in accordance with the tenancy and a landlord should exercise great caution before evicting you without a court order (see chapter 3).

In all the above cases, the law is complex and you should always take legal advice. See chapter 8 for more information.

Oral agreements – are they binding?

It is not uncommon for a student to move into a property without having signed a written contract.

It may be in such cases that a contract has been given to the occupier but they don't sign before moving in. In some cases, however, no written contract exists at all. In these circumstances what is known as an 'oral agreement' applies.

Is an oral agreement binding? In general, yes. The law does not usually require tenancy or licence agreements to be in writing (there are exceptions concerning some types of long term tenancy, particularly fixed-term leases for three years or more, but they are very unlikely to affect students). However, establishing the legal consequences of an oral agreement is more difficult.

- The agreement is much more likely to be a tenancy than a licence. Except in the self evident cases like hotels and hostels, licences need to be specifically created and the 'fall back' position is a tenancy.

- What type of tenancy it is depends largely on who the landlord is. In the case of private landlords, since 28th February 1997 any tenancy, written or oral, is an assured shorthold unless the landlord states otherwise.

- In the somewhat unlikely situation that you went into possession of the property before 28th February 1997 (the date when the relevant parts of the Housing Act 1996 came into force) you might find that you have better legal rights. This is because most written agreements would have been offered as assured shorthold tenancies – whereas your status under the oral agreement would be as an assured tenant.

- The tenancy will be a periodic rather than a fixed term one (this is explained below) because fixed term tenancies need to be specifically created. The type of periodic tenancy will depend upon the manner in which rent is paid: if paid weekly it will be a weekly tenancy, if paid monthly, a monthly tenancy, and so on.

- The issue of whether you are a sole or joint tenant will depend upon questions like whether you approached the landlord or their agent as a group and how rent is paid (see page 17 for further information).

Working out the terms of an oral tenancy is difficult. You might think there are no 'terms' because nothing is in writing. However, a contractual term can be 'implied' as well as 'express', so that an apparently blank oral agreement can be filled out with terms to a degree. Some terms are implied by statute, for example the term as to landlords' repairing obligations contained in s.11 of the Landlord and Tenant Act 1985 (see chapter 5). If there is a written agreement but you didn't sign it before moving in, it may be that terms from the written agreement will be implied into your oral agreement.

(This is not certain and if it is important please take legal advice.)

Other terms are implied as a result of what is a normal expectation of an agreement of that type (see for example the obligation of a tenant to act in a 'tenant-like' manner, also discussed in chapter 5).

Whether it is wise to move in without a signed contract is more doubtful. Your legal position is definitely less clear, particularly when considering the detailed terms under which you occupy. Also you have to ask yourself why no written agreement was produced by the landlord – might it suggest that there is something you should worry about, for example, that they have a mortgage on the property which prohibits tenancies?

In a few cases it may not be clear to you whether your agreement is in writing or not. Perhaps the two commonest situations are:

• agreements made electronically

• written agreements which are never signed.

As regards electronic agreements (which are becoming increasingly common in relation to landlords who let on a large scale to students) the best analysis is probably that information on a web site or similar about available accommodation is what is normally termed an invitation to treat (an invitation to others to make offers). If you then make an application for particular accommodation advertised this way you are offering to live there on the basis of the terms and other details laid out on the web site. Once the landlord accepts your application there is then a contract based on these written details.

If subsequently you are sent a tenancy agreement to sign and return, make sure you check it first. If you find the written agreement contains additional information or obligations you are not happy with, take advice before signing and returning. It may be that you are not legally bound by these extra provisos.

As regards written agreements which are never signed, the best analysis is probably that you have agreed to the written terms in the agreement given to you by your conduct in moving into the property and continuing to live there without objecting to the terms and/or proposing alternatives.

3

Subjects covered in this chapter include...

What 'quiet enjoyment' means

When the landlord can enter your home

Should the landlord have a key?

Harassment and unlawful eviction

What you can do about it

All occupiers are entitled to use their accommodation without undue interference by their landlord. In most cases, the landlord is not entitled to enter your accommodation without your permission. While the law does not differentiate between different types of landlord, in practice private landlords are most likely to cause problems here. Unacceptable behaviour can range from the annoying to the drastic:

- *entering the accommodation while you are out*

- *trying to restrict your enjoyment of the accommodation*

- *cutting off electricity or other supplies*

- *harassing you in subtle (or not so subtle) ways*

- *putting all your possessions in black bin bags and changing the locks.*

Such behaviour can arise where landlords still see the accommodation as their own and are not prepared to take any notice of your contractual or legal rights; or where they are unaware that you have any rights. It often begins when there is a dispute about rent or how the accommodation is being used.

Low level problems are best resolved by communicating in person with the landlord as quickly as possible. If this does not work, bringing in a third party such as the university or college accommodation service to mediate may help. Cases that are more serious could require the involvement of the Citizens Advice Bureau (CAB), a Shelter housing adviser, a solicitor or the local authority. Frequently (and understandably), students simply leave and find new accommodation, but this does not resolve the problem for future occupiers.

Quiet enjoyment

All tenants are entitled to 'quiet enjoyment' of their accommodation through their contract with the landlord. This may be specifically included in the tenancy agreement but the law implies it in any event. It is very difficult to define quiet enjoyment: most definitions focus on lists of behaviour. The word 'quiet' does not specifically relate to noise – though quiet enjoyment can certainly cover noise. Quiet enjoyment relates to your fundamental entitlement to use your accommodation without interference.

In serious cases that have reached the courts, the following have all been found to represent a breach of this right:

- landlord threatened tenant through letters and by shouting and banging on tenant's door
- landlord changed lock
- cutting off mains services
- landlord spat in tenant's face, and then broke door lock and removed tenant's possessions while tenant was reporting the matter to the police
- a tenant with an assured shorthold who was on holiday was locked out by the landlord
- carrying out building works which caused noise and loss of privacy.

The following have been found not to be a breach:

- failure to carry out repairs (but failure to deal with the consequences of disrepair can be a breach)
- letting property with poor sound insulation (though noise that seriously interferes with a tenant's enjoyment of the property can be).

The right to quiet enjoyment does not automatically apply to students who are licensees though they do have some protection. In a 1981 case, students in Sandby Hall, a hall of residence in Nottingham, complained that it was almost impossible to prepare for exams in their study bedrooms due to the noise made by repair work that the university was carrying out. The court said that the university should do nothing without just cause to disturb the students from getting on with their studies with 'reasonable quietude' in their rooms (*Smith v. Nottinghamshire County Council* (1981) The Times 13 November). This suggests that the university could have carried out emergency work but not disruptive repairs, which could have waited until after exams had finished or the end of term.

Case

A group of students approached the university Accommodation Office when they found the service provided by their landlord too good! In response to repair requests he would carry out repairs himself, but sit down for a cup of tea and chat when he had finished, and then look around the property to find other (non essential) repairs to carry out, and come back shortly to carry them out and to have another chat... The students did not like to complain as the landlord was a nice fellow, but he really did outstay his welcome and interfere with their 'quiet enjoyment'.

The Accommodation Office contacted the landlord, who was shocked to find his visits were unwelcome. A few weeks later he contacted the university and asked it to put the property in its management scheme, which it agreed to do.

Comment

While this scenario may initially appear to be a minor problem, it does highlight the basic fact that tenants are entitled to their own space. The student rental market attracts landlords both large and small, who sometimes do not understand their responsibilities. At one extreme repair requests may be ignored and, at the other, landlords may treat the property as their own and refuse to 'let go'.

Trespassing

Landlords have no general right to enter tenants' rooms. This is because tenants have exclusive possession of their accommodation. To overcome this problem, tenancy agreements usually contain clauses that give the landlord a right to enter. In the typical example quoted below, the landlord's rights are restricted and any entry outside its terms would be a trespass. Emergency access, for example, to fix a burst pipe while you were away, would not be a trespass.

Example of tenancy agreement clause

'Allow entry by the landlord and agent

The tenant will allow the landlord at all reasonable times to enter the premises for the purpose of:

- *repairing or painting the outside of the premises*

- *carrying out any structural or other necessary repairs to the premises*

- *examining the state and condition of the premises, or*

- *(in the last three months) showing the premises to prospective tenants or purchasers.'*

In this clause, the term 'landlord' includes the landlord's agent, any superior landlord and, where necessary, workmen and others. The landlord must give reasonable prior notice of his intention to enter the premises during the tenancy period. In the event of an emergency, notice may not be required.

Where you have a genuine licence agreement, this may well give the landlord a more general right to enter your accommodation, for example, to clean the room.

Keys

Difficulties about keys to rooms can arise in this context. Landlords frequently retain keys. This may be so that they can enter the premises to provide services such as changing bed linen or cleaning or for access in an emergency. However, if you are concerned about security, you might want to change a lock. If there is a common entrance shared with other occupiers of the property, you cannot change this lock without the consent of the other occupiers and the landlord. As far as your own room is concerned, you do have the right to change the lock by, for example, changing the barrel of a Yale lock. Your tenancy agreement may seek to forbid this or require you to provide a new key to the landlord. You should consider your housing status in chapter 8 to consider possible consequences as failing to comply with the tenancy agreement could lead to the landlord seeking to evict you.

Personal possessions

In all situations, landlords should not interfere with your personal possessions. To do so would also constitute trespass. In one horrendous reported case, a landlord burned a student's PhD notes (*Caruso v. Owen* 1983).

Harassment and unlawful eviction

Under the Protection from Eviction Act 1977, tenants and most licensees have the legal right not to be harassed or unlawfully evicted by their landlord. Harassment and unlawful eviction can give rise to both a right to compensation from the landlord and criminal proceedings being taken against the landlord.

Harassment is defined as

- doing acts likely to interfere with a residential occupier's peace or comfort, or

- persistently withdrawing or withholding services.

One example would be the landlord refusing to allow you to use facilities that are part of your letting agreement. If it was agreed that you could use a washing machine located in a separate room, the landlord cannot unilaterally withdraw that right later. This would also apply to rights to use facilities such as a shared kitchen, bathroom, garden or shed. Cutting off your gas or electricity supply could constitute harassment even if there is a dispute about bills.

Unlawful eviction is committed where a landlord unlawfully deprives a residential occupier of any premises. An eviction is unlawful where a landlord has evicted an occupier without going through the correct notice and court procedures (see chapter 8). This would be the case even if the occupier had not paid their rent or had broken the terms of the licence or tenancy agreement. One of the clearest examples would be a landlord unilaterally changing your lock so that you cannot get in. Refusing to replace a tenant's lost key has also been held to constitute unlawful eviction.

Tenancy agreements frequently contain forfeiture clauses, which say that the landlord can 're-enter' the accommodation and end the tenancy where the occupier has broken its terms. Landlords should be aware that the law frequently requires the service of notices and the obtaining of a court possession order. Without them, the eviction will be unlawful despite the forfeiture clause.

Remedies

Where a landlord's behaviour falls into any of the categories above, you have a number of options:

- seeking to get the harassment stopped
- seeking compensation from the landlord for his/her bad behaviour
- recovering your possessions
- getting back into your accommodation
- getting the landlord prosecuted.

Where difficulties arise, you should keep a diary detailing what happened and when. This will be useful as evidence should matters get worse. Many students worry about making complaints because they think this will lead to further problems with the landlord but 'putting up with it' can also lead to landlords assuming that they can do what they like. You should seek advice and support from the university or college accommodation service. A complaint can be made to the local housing authority's Tenancy Relations Officer (TRO). The TRO's role is to make a landlord comply with the law. However, many TROs see their role as conciliating between landlords and tenants when disputes arise and they will try to calm things down by talking to both parties. See chapter 9 ('Further advice and contacts') for more information about TROs.

Where the situation has become serious, all but the last option are likely to involve the occupier in having to instruct a lawyer to take civil proceedings against the landlord. A court action can seek all these remedies. Experienced solicitors can act very quickly to get court orders, which will order the landlord to return your possessions and let you back in, and restrain the landlord from harassing you. A landlord who does not comply with an order can be brought before the court for contempt.

Obtaining damages (compensation) from the landlord will take longer but it is worth bearing in mind that this kind of behaviour can be taken very seriously by the courts. See the example below.

> In the case of *Dimoutsikou v. Penrose* (Leeds County Court, 17.5.2000) a tenant who had an assured shorthold tenancy was locked out while on holiday. The court decided that the landlord had deliberately acted while the tenant was away. It ordered the landlord to pay the tenant a total of £8,438.40 damages.

The normal way of calculating damages in these cases is to compensate the tenant for losses resulting from the harassment or illegal eviction. This could include:

- damage to or loss of personal belongings

- additional housing costs incurred

- legal costs.

A much higher level of damages can be awarded under section 28 of the Housing Act 1988. This is based on what the landlord has gained by evicting the tenant i.e. the difference between the value of the property with the tenant there and the value of the property without the tenant. See the example below.

> In *Tagro v. Cafane* [1991] (Lambeth County Court 24.11.89), the landlord and his agent changed the locks to the tenant's flat. The tenant had to get two injunctions to get back in and then found the flat ransacked and his belongings gone. The court awarded £31,000 damages under s.28 plus £15,538 compensation for damage to and loss of possessions.

The amount of compensation available under section 28 will depend on the nature of the property. If you are the only occupier of a property, it could be quite high. If you are, for example, only one of a number of occupiers of bedsits in a large property, the difference between the value of the whole property with and without your presence could be small.

Further rules say that this basis of calculation does not apply at all

- if the tenant is reinstated before the completion of civil proceedings,

  or

- if the landlord believed (and had reasonable cause to believe) that the tenant had left the premises.

The amount of damages can be reduced if the tenant's conduct or that of anyone living with him or her before the eviction was 'such that it is reasonable to mitigate the damages'. The suggestion here is that in some circumstances tenants may have brought or partly brought the problem on themselves by breaking the terms of the tenancy agreement. This might be the case where the tenant has behaved in an anti-social way towards the landlord or other occupiers.

The damages can also be reduced if the landlord offers to re-instate the tenant before proceedings are begun and it was unreasonable of the tenant to refuse the offer.

Prosecutions

In serious cases of harassment and unlawful eviction, local authorities can prosecute landlords. The maximum penalties are an unlimited fine and/or two years imprisonment. In practice, this forms part of the work of TROs. As noted above, many TROs see their role as conciliatory and they are reluctant to prosecute. Consequently, there are considerable variations in practice between authorities.

Generally, there are few prosecutions other than in exceptionally serious cases (see example below). Some of the reasons given by authorities for their reluctance are

- the tenant's fear of reprisals and reluctance to go to court
- difficulty with evidence (lack of corroboration and detailed records)
- the time it takes to get to court
- the high burden of proof required in criminal cases
- the cost of assembling and prosecuting the case.

However, a well organised and well publicised case can effectively deter local landlords from indulging in this kind of illegal behaviour.

Case

In October 2000, Tony Carroll, a Nottingham landlord, removed the back door of a property let to Nottingham University students with a crowbar, and did not replace it for some days afterwards.

There was a dispute over rent. According to the landlord, he had agreed to allow the students to live in the house over the summer, but they moved in earlier than agreed and then claimed that they owed no rent for September.

Carroll, who had 20 rented properties, was reported as saying: 'I took the door off as a way of upsetting them. The only other way to deal with these issues is to go through the courts, which can take a long time, and get you nowhere. Normally I love renting to students.'

As a result of the landlord's actions, most of the students had to leave to live in emergency accommodation and one student was so distressed that he had to postpone his studies, returning to live with his parents.

Nottingham City Council brought a prosecution against the landlord under the Protection from Eviction Act. In March 2002, Nottingham Magistrates Court found that the landlord had broken the law and that as a result of the incidents the tenants had been forced to give up possession of the premises. He was fined £1,000 and ordered to pay £500 costs.

Source: Nottingham City Council and Residential Property Investor (April/May 2002)

Subjects covered in this chapter include...

When the rent can be increased

How to challenge the rent

Deposits and premiums

When a rent guarantor is necessary

Liability for Council Tax

Eligibility for Council Tax Benefit and Housing Benefit

Whether you live in a hall of residence, rent from a private landlord, or have any kind of 'social' tenancy, one thing is constant – you have to pay to live there!

What you pay may be described as rent or as a licence charge or fee.

The amount you agree to pay at the outset may be increased even while you are living there, or (in a few cases) you may be able to get it reduced.

You may be asked to pay a premium before you are allowed to move in. (A premium is, effectively, a charge made for allocating the property to you.)

You will normally be asked to pay some kind of deposit before you move in (though you may get the full deposit back when you leave).

If you leave the property before the law allows you to, or without giving any notice due, you will normally be liable to your landlord for any outstanding rent or licence charges.

If you are a joint tenant, you will normally be liable for any unpaid rent on the property jointly occupied and not just for your own share of the rent.

If the whole property you live in is occupied by students, or if you live in a hall of residence, you should not be liable to Council Tax.

If you are liable, in a few cases you may be eligible for Council Tax Benefit.

Finally, in situations similar to those where Council Tax Benefit (CTB) is payable, you may be eligible for Housing Benefit (HB) to help with the rent. Unfortunately most students do not qualify.

What is rent?

Simply, it is the payment which a tenant is bound by contract to make to their landlord for the exclusive possession of the property let. In almost all student tenancies there will be a rent to be paid, and it will be expressed in money terms (although strictly a tenancy can exist without a rent being payable).

Before moving in, check the following (ideally your landlord or their letting agent should confirm in writing).

• How much rent is payable and what it includes – for example, if it includes any other bills such as gas, electricity, water, telephone charges or Council Tax (although in the case of student tenancies it should not include the latter).

- When you are due to pay. Rent is usually paid weekly, monthly, or termly in advance, with the first payment due when you move in.

- How you should pay. You may be asked to pay by cheque, by cash, by credit card or even by standing order or direct debit. If you pay cash, always make sure you are given a receipt. Your landlord may ask for post-dated cheques in advance to cover future rent. This is particularly likely where rent is paid termly. Although banks disapprove of this practice, it is legal. You must decide how comfortable you feel about this (and don't forget that a fee will be payable to your bank if you subsequently cancel a cheque).

- Whether there are any clauses in your tenancy agreement which allow the rent to be increased (this is discussed further below).

The following are *not* rent:

- Breakage deposits (see below). These may be expressed as a multiple of the rent you pay. They should not be confused with payments of rent in advance, which some landlords also demand.

- Premiums for the grant of the tenancy (see below).

- Service or utility charges (such as gas, water, electricity or telephone bills).

- Council Tax (although as a student you are generally not liable to pay this: see below).

- Licence charges/payments.

- Payments made to your landlord after your tenancy has come to an end and when you do not have a continuing right to remain in the property. These are normally referred to as mesne profits.

How important is it that these payments are not rent? On a practical level, it is important to distinguish premiums, deposits and service charges from rent. Also, deposits for breakage, premiums, and service/utility charges are not 'eligible rent' for Housing Benefit purposes in those cases where students can claim Housing Benefit. If you become potentially vulnerable to eviction for non-payment of rent (see chapter 8) it is important to check whether any or all of the debt due relates to rent. For present purposes it is not particularly significant whether what you pay to your landlord is (strictly) rent or is a licence fee, or 'mesne profits'. All of these are 'eligible rent' for Housing Benefit purposes (although whether something is rent or 'mesne profits' can be very important as regards implying a new tenancy by acceptance of rent by your landlord).

Should I have a rent book?

If you pay your rent weekly you must have a rent book unless your rent includes a substantial proportion for food and other services. If you do have to have a rent book it should include:

- the name and address of your landlord and of the landlord's agent, if they have one
- the rent payable
- information about your rights to protection from eviction
- information about agencies which can give you further advice.

If your landlord fails to supply you with an appropriate rent book when it is a legal requirement they are guilty of a criminal offence.

Of course, a rent book is, above all, evidence of the rent you have paid. If you have one, make sure it is kept up to date by your landlord. If you don't have one, but you should have one by law, make sure you get one. If you don't have one, and there is no legal obligation on your landlord to provide one, then always try to get something in writing from the landlord or their agent acknowledging that you have paid.

Caution in advance can avoid difficulties later over claims of unpaid rent.

If no rent book is needed (most students pay their rent monthly or termly so there is no legal requirement to provide one) the amount of rent and method of payment should be clearly indicated in your tenancy (or licence) agreement. (This assumes, of course, that you have a written agreement!) If it isn't, you should ask the landlord about this and press them for something in writing.

In any event, if you have an assured shorthold tenancy (see chapter 2) which began on or after 28th February 1997 and you have no written agreement, or your agreement does not contain details of rent, you have a right to request a written statement of the following:

- the amount of rent payable and when it should be paid
- any arrangements for increasing the rent
- the date your tenancy began and the length of any fixed term.

It is illegal for your landlord not to provide you with such a statement within 28 days of receiving your request in writing (s.20A of the Housing Act 1988, as amended).

Increasing the rent payable

The first thing to do is to check whether your tenancy (or licence) agreement specifies any procedure for your rent to be increased. Unless the agreement contains a clause allowing your landlord to increase the rent, they can only do so if:

• you agree to any increase

or

• they have a statutory right to increase the rent (see below).

If there is a clause allowing the rent to be increased (often termed a rent review clause) read through it carefully and if necessary have it checked out legally. You should think very carefully before signing the agreement if you are unhappy with anything the agreement says about increasing your rent.

Most students have assured shorthold tenancies (AST). In the case of an AST the landlord will not be able to increase the rent in the first six months of the tenancy or, if it is a fixed term tenancy, for the duration of the initial fixed term. After this, it all depends on whether you simply carry on in possession or whether you sign a new agreement. In the former case the rules are much the same as for assured tenancies. In the latter case you are bound to pay the rent laid down in the new agreement.

In the case of assured tenancies (see chapter 2) it is possible that there will be a rent review clause allowing rent to be increased even during the initial period of the tenancy (i.e. before the end of any fixed term). Always check for this. Otherwise a landlord's right to increase rent depends on whether the tenancy is fixed term or periodic (see chapter 2).

If it is fixed term, the rent cannot be increased until the fixed term expires, and a statutory periodic tenancy (see chapter 8) comes into being (s.13 of the Housing Act 1988).

If it is periodic the rent can be increased by the service of a notice by the landlord under s.13 once one year has passed from the beginning of the tenancy.

The procedure your landlord has to use to increase your rent under s.13 is complicated, but in outline they have to serve a notice of increase on you (giving you at least a month's warning). If you are unhappy with the proposed increase, you can refer it to the appropriate local Rent Assessment Committee (RAC). The RAC is usually made up of three people – a lawyer, a property valuer and a lay person. In the case of a s.13 notice of increase, their job is to decide whether the increased rent proposed by your landlord is in line with what would generally be expected in the area.

Always get advice before making an application to the RAC. It may be possible to be legally represented before the committee (see also chapter 9).

Remember that all the above assumes that there is no rent review clause in your original tenancy agreement. If there is, it takes precedence over anything in s.13 (s.13(1)(b)). Also, if your landlord persuades you to voluntarily accept a rent increase this is legally binding (s.13(5)). So think very hard before agreeing to any such proposal and take advice if you have any doubts.

As regards council tenancies, local authorities have very wide powers to review rents regularly and impose 'reasonable' charges. Challenging this is a difficult and uncertain process. Always seek advice first.

If you have a protected or statutory Rent Act tenancy (see chapter 2) your landlord's ability to increase rents is very tightly controlled by law. Students are very unlikely to have such a tenancy as, in general, you have to have been continuously in possession of your property since before 15th January 1989 to qualify. Space does not permit a full examination here of the complex issues of rent and Rent Act tenancies – it is important to seek advice.

Finally, there are no distinct statutory rules concerning licences and non assured tenancies. Everything depends on what is stated in the agreement. If, for example, there is nothing in the agreement on increasing licence charges, it is safe to assume they cannot be increased for the duration of the agreement.

Challenging the rent

If you are unhappy with a proposed rent the obvious advice is not to enter into the agreement. In general you are bound by the rent once you have 'signed up'. This is definitely the case with non assured/non secure tenancies, licences, council tenancies and assured tenancies.

As regards assured shorthold tenancies, you can apply to the RAC at the beginning of your tenancy if you think your rent is excessive compared to rents on similar properties in the area. The RAC will only decide to change your rent if there are enough assured shorthold tenancies in the area with which to compare it, and they think your existing rent is considerably higher than rents for similar properties (s.22 of the

Housing Act 1988). There is no right to apply to the RAC concerning any 'follow up' ASTs. If your AST began at any time from 28th February 1997 onwards you have a right to apply to the RAC during the first six months of the tenancy (s.22(2)(aa) of the Housing Act 1988).

If you are considering referring your AST rent to the RAC please bear the following points in mind:

The RAC will only reduce your rent if it is clearly excessive. Check carefully with other students you know who live in similar properties in the same area.

As an assured shorthold tenant you have very limited security (see chapters 2 and 8). Your landlord could decide to evict you lawfully when your tenancy agreement ends if you choose to challenge the rent.

So, if you like the property and would like to carry on living there when your current agreement ends you have to consider whether challenging the rent is worth it, even if it does seem a little high.

If you think you have a Rent Act statutory or periodic tenancy take advice immediately. Your rent is subject to strict statutory 'fair rent' controls via the Rent Officer and Rent Assessment Committee.

Deposits and premiums

Most landlords, particularly private landlords, ask new tenants to pay a deposit, although they are not legally obliged to do so. Although there is no legal limit on the amount of a deposit the most common figure is one or two months' rent. In addition, you may be asked to pay rent in advance, and/or some kind of charge for granting you the tenancy. This is often called a premium. Increasingly students are asked to pay holding deposits, also known as retainers, to secure the property prior to final signing of contracts and/or moving in.

Deposits

The deposit which private landlords almost invariably ask you to pay is intended to give them some financial security against any financial loss they may suffer as a result of any damage you may cause to the property. It may even be termed a 'breakage deposit' or 'damage deposit' in the agreement, although these terms have no special legal significance.

Unfortunately the issue of deposits and, in particular, their non-return by landlords at the end of the agreement is a major source of dispute and friction. Some landlords seem to regard a deposit as extra rent, only to be returned reluctantly.

Keep the following points in mind:

- Before you agree to pay a deposit you should ask the landlord to confirm in writing exactly what the deposit covers and when the money will be returned to you. Always ask for a receipt for any deposit paid.

- Try to ensure your landlord gives you an inventory (a list of the contents and condition of the property) before you move in. Check this carefully to make sure it is accurate and that everything is in working order. Then, if possible, agree the inventory with the landlord.

- If you don't receive an inventory, write one yourself with an independent witness, such as a friend, and send a copy to your landlord/agent. It might be a good idea to get this witness to sign and date that the inventory is a true record of the condition of the property. It may even be helpful to take photographs to record the condition of the property when you move in, perhaps even dated by (for example) a suitably placed newspaper in the photograph! Keep this record up to date during the agreement.

- Make a careful note of the state of decoration of the property, and the condition of any furniture and appliances supplied. If anything is worn, broken, or damaged report this in writing to your landlord and keep a copy.

If you do all the above this will make things much easier if any dispute arises at the end of your agreement over the return of your deposit. Nevertheless, problems may still arise. Ideally your landlord (or their agent) should hold your deposit in a separate client account, and pay you interest on the deposit when it is returned to you (at all times it remains your money). In a few cases your landlord may have joined the Tenancy Deposit scheme currently being piloted by the Government (see chapter 9 for more information).

Unfortunately, none of this is legally required. If a dispute does arise concerning the return of your deposit, bear the following in mind.

- The onus is on your landlord to prove that there are circumstances justifying their retention of all (or part) of your deposit, not for you to prove that you are entitled to its return.

- Your landlord cannot withhold your deposit because of general 'wear and tear' while you have been living in the property. Landlords will be expected to redecorate and replace carpets and furnishings every few years – perhaps even more frequently if there is a high turnover of tenants. You should only be held liable for any damage which creates additional costs for your landlord.

- If you leave the property still owing rent to your landlord they will, in practice, be able to keep back any part of your deposit corresponding to the rent owing. It is debatable whether it is technically correct to view unpaid rent as payable from the deposit. However, if you were to sue the landlord for the return of your deposit (below) they could in return sue you for unpaid rent (this is called a counter claim).

- If you move out leaving unpaid bills for water, gas, electricity or telephone charges it will generally be up to the relevant company to pursue you (if you are the one named on the agreement with them), and possibly other users, for the debt. Your landlord should not deduct money from your deposit to cover bills unless the bills remained in their name or they suffered other financial loss as a result, for example in having to pay for services to be reconnected. In this type of case you should seek advice.

If you do need to take legal action to recover your deposit, always seek advice first. It may be that simple legal pressure will be enough but, unfortunately, in some cases a small claim in the County Court may be needed (see also chapter 9). You will not be able to get legal aid for someone to represent you in such a claim but some of the organisations listed in chapter 9, or your Students' Union, may be able to represent you.

Case

Mr Lloyd rented a property to the local university who sublet it to six students as part of their 'head tenancy' management scheme. This arrangement ended after six years as the university required properties closer to its campus. After the last group of tenants moved out, the owner claimed a total of £410 for damage to the property. The university held a damage deposit of £150 for each student.

The claim included items that were rejected by the university because they were attributable to fair wear and tear e.g. damage to an electric socket, a new rubber door seal for the fridge, and minor damage to the face of a bedroom door.

A substantial part of the claim related to damage to a three piece suite caused by a hot object being placed on it. The university felt the claim was unreasonable as the furniture in the house consisted of a variety of long serving and second hand units, with very little furniture that matched. However, the damage to the armchair was quite bad and had been noticed during a routine inspection, and the student responsible was known. The university agreed to refund £120 for a new chair less 25% for wear and tear, i.e. £90.

Hence, of the owner's original claim for £410, only £115 was refunded, and of this only £90 was deducted from the deposit of the student responsible for the damage to the chair.

Comment

Although the university was managing the property and could moderate unreasonable demands from the owner, this case does demonstrate how claims for damage should be reasonable. This is significant in high turnover, multi-occupied properties where heavy usage should be expected, especially if furniture and fittings are not particularly robust and/or second hand.

If the students had been renting directly from the landlord, they could have sought advice from the university or another advice agency to challenge the claim. Ultimately, if the landlord had actually withheld the deposits, they could have taken action in the Small Claims Court to seek a refund for the reasons stated. It is also important that efforts are made to charge the person actually responsible for the damage. In this case, although a communal armchair had been damaged, it would have been unreasonable to apportion costs to all tenants when only one was responsible.

Premiums

In the unlikely event that you have a Rent Act tenancy, it is illegal for you to be charged a fee (often called a premium) simply for the privilege of being granted the tenancy (see s.119 of the Rent Act 1977). However, premiums can be validly charged in relation to other tenancies or licence agreements. The practice is not very common in relation to student tenancies and licences. If you are asked to pay a premium (which is non-returnable at the end of the agreement) it may cause you to think twice about entering into the agreement, particularly if the sum involved is substantial. Also, be careful to check whether you are being asked to pay a premium, or simply rent in advance (or both). Paying rent in advance simply means that no rent should be owing from you at the end of the tenancy (although it may weaken your tactical position concerning disrepair if you do pay rent in advance – see chapter 5 – and if you do qualify for Housing Benefit this is paid in arrears – see below).

Accommodation agency charges

It is illegal for an accommodation agency to charge you a fee simply for putting you on their books, or supplying you with a list of possible accommodation.

Retainers

Whereas it is relatively uncommon for students to be asked to pay a premium, it is relatively common for them to be asked to pay a retainer or holding deposit. The reason for this is that students commonly look for properties in the period from March to June each year, while only intending to move in from September. There is nothing unlawful about being asked to pay a retainer but, unfortunately, the legal implications of doing so are far from clear.

One interpretation is that the retainer is simply a charge for the eventual 'grant' of the tenancy (in other words it is, effectively, a premium, and so non-refundable). This may be plausible in some cases but seems an unlikely interpretation if the retainer is expressed as a weekly charge covering the period between signing the agreement and moving in.

Another interpretation is that the retainer is a payment for a guarantee that you will be granted the tenancy (i.e. it is a kind of 'option' over it). In such a case the retainer would only be refundable if you go ahead. Again, if the 'retainer' is expressed as a weekly charge covering the period after signature it cannot be seen as merely the acquiring of an option, if for no other reason than that both parties are legally bound by the contract once it is signed.

Finally, a payment described as a retainer or holding deposit may, in fact, be rent covering the initial period of the tenancy. It is not uncommon to find a clause that half the rent needs to be paid from the period the agreement is signed until some later date (typically near the start of the next academic year) when the full rent 'kicks in'. This could be viewed as the creation of a tenancy, with all its attendant rights and duties on both sides, from the date of signature. If so, you would be entitled to use the property, and claim exclusive possession over it from this date. In our experience the issue is not merely academic, particularly as it is not unknown for landlords to fill up the property with another short term occupant prior to the date when full rent becomes payable. If a tenancy does exist, the landlord who did this would be in breach of the covenant of quiet enjoyment (see chapter 3).

There seems to be no case law on this issue and our view is open to debate. You should clarify with your landlord what rights they intend you to acquire by paying the retainer, and get their response in writing. If you are not happy with the response, our advice is not to go ahead. If a dispute arises later, take legal advice.

The obligation to pay rent

Your principal obligation as a tenant is to pay your rent (or licence charge) as and when it becomes due. If you fall into arrears you become liable to eviction, even in cases where otherwise you have legal security although, in general, rent arrears are not automatic 'grounds for possession' (all this is discussed in detail in chapter 8). Before you are vulnerable to a rent arrears 'ground' the rent must be 'lawfully due'. In part this relates to the relevant legal date for arrears to be outstanding (again, see chapter 8) but also concerns the obligation of a landlord to give their tenants an address at which notices (including all legal notices) need to be served on them. If a landlord fails to provide this, rent is not regarded as being 'lawfully due' (see s.48 of the Landlord and Tenant Act 1987). So, if your landlord has not given you their name and address they will not be able to enforce any rent demands against you. You will typically expect to find this address in the tenancy agreement, or in the rent book if there is one.

Problems which can arise in relation to (claimed) rent arrears include:

• Your landlord may refuse to accept rent from you. This is most likely to arise if there is a dispute between you. To protect yourself in such a case you should write to your landlord stating you wish to pay the rent. Keep a copy of this letter. Then, set up a bank or building society account and pay your rent into it, so that you have the money to pay when your landlord eventually agrees to accept it (or takes you to court on grounds of rent arrears).

- You do not have an automatic right to withhold rent if your landlord does not carry out or refuses to carry out repairs on the property. However, you may be able to do the repairs yourself and deduct the cost from future rent. This is discussed in more detail in chapter 5.

If you leave the property before the end of a fixed term tenancy or licence where there is no right to terminate early, or fail to give appropriate notice to quit or terminate the agreement even in cases (fixed term or periodic) where you can terminate early, you are legally obliged to pay rent until the end of the fixed term or the point when adequate notice would have expired. (The mechanics of giving notice are discussed in chapter 8.) Even after you have physically left the property you still owe this unpaid rent to your ex-landlord as a debt and they can sue you for it in the County Court. However your landlord is under a duty to attempt to re-let the property and if another tenant or licensee enters into an agreement to move in, your liability ends at that point.

If you can, avoid 'walking out' on an agreement owing rent. Even if you find living in the property difficult, perhaps because of the other residents, try to negotiate some kind of compromise with your landlord rather than simply leaving. Some of the organisations mentioned in chapter 9 may be able to help.

If you are a joint tenant (see chapter 2) you are liable for the whole rent due on the property, in conjunction with the other joint tenants. If one of you leaves early owing rent, your landlord can choose to require those remaining to cover the sums outstanding rather than go after the tenant who has left. If you find yourself in this situation you can in theory seek recompense from the joint tenant who left, but this is legally difficult and you should always seek advice.

Rent guarantors

It is becoming increasingly common for landlords to want your parents or someone similar to 'underwrite' your rent. If you are under 18 (see chapter 2) this is almost always the case. In legal terms, if you contract to occupy property as a tenant or licensee you are the major potential debtor and your landlord can always look to you for unpaid rent. However, if you are unable, or unwilling, to pay they may seek to enforce the debt against any person who has 'guaranteed' it.

Rent undertaking – liability of guarantors

A guarantor is only liable to pay if the main debtor is also liable. So if, for any reason, the main tenancy or licence contract is unenforceable then the guarantee is unenforceable as well.

A guarantee is only enforceable if it is either in writing or there is some written evidence of it, and, it has been signed by the guarantor or their agent.

A guarantee may on closer examination not be a guarantee at all, but rather what is termed an 'indemnity'. This is important because in theory a verbal indemnity is enforceable.

What is the difference between a rent undertaking guarantee and an indemnity?

The simple, but rather unhelpful, answer is that it depends on what the parties intend. In practice it will depend on the words used. If the agreement seems to underwrite the debt come what may it is an indemnity, while if it merely promises to pay if the main debtor is liable to pay and fails to do so it is a guarantee.

In general, you will usually be liable for any rent commitment you have given, so that your rent guarantor will be liable whether they have technically made a guarantee or an indemnity.

Also note that if your parent or other rent guarantor does have to underwrite your rent they can in theory pursue you for what they have had to pay out!

Council Tax

If you are a full-time student living in a property where all the residents are students, or if you are living in a hall of residence, you are not liable to pay Council Tax (you live in an 'exempt dwelling'). 'Full-time student' in relation to Council Tax means someone undertaking a full-time course of further or higher education. A 'full-time course' means a course which requires study and tuition amounting to at least 21 hours per week for at least 24 weeks in the year.

Therefore, you probably will not have to pay Council Tax, although it may be necessary in the case of private sector accommodation to ensure that 'exemption' is acknowledged by the council. You may need to send them exemption certificates for all occupants – obtainable from your university or college. However, given that liability will sometimes arise (below) the nature of Council Tax is summarised here.

This summary is only an outline and should not be taken to be a comprehensive statement of the law. If you need to look into it further, a good reference point is *Council Tax Handbook* by Martin Ward, published by the Child Poverty Action Group.

- Council Tax (which replaced the community charge, or 'poll tax' on 1st April 1993) is a tax on residential properties (referred to as 'dwellings'). It is the means by which local people pay towards the cost of providing local services, such as street cleaning, refuse collection, education and social services.

- Liability for the tax arises on a daily basis.

- 'Dwellings' includes houses, flats and bed-sits, whether lived in or not. It can even include houseboats and mobile homes.

- There is one Council Tax bill for each dwelling but a number of people may be responsible for paying it (for example resident joint tenants).

- All dwellings are placed in one of eight valuation bands according to their assumed market value. The lower the valuation band, the lower the tax.

- In addition to wholly student occupied properties and halls of residence, there are other 'exempt dwellings', for example an unoccupied dwelling which has been repossessed by a mortgage lender, and dwellings which are exempt for up to six months, for example a largely unfurnished dwelling which has undergone major repairs or structural alterations.

Situations where students may be liable to pay Council Tax

- Where they are part-time rather than full-time students.

- Where the dwelling they live in is not wholly occupied by students. This can cause difficulties, particularly where a student leaves part way through a year (perhaps because they have left their course) and is replaced by someone who is not a full-time student. This will then normally 'trigger' liability for Council Tax from that point onwards. The local authority may only identify this later and then pursue everyone for Council Tax arrears.

  If you feel you may be in this kind of situation, always take advice.

Consequences of the dwelling ceasing to be exempt

Council Tax is potentially payable by all those residents in the dwelling. There is, however, a 'hierarchy' of liability. In order of priority this includes:

- a resident owner

- a resident tenant

- a resident sub-tenant

- a resident licensee.

So a licensee (see chapter 2) will only be liable to pay if there are no tenants or sub-tenants residing in the same dwelling. If there are a number of residents with the same status, they are jointly liable.

The main implications of this for students who are not exempt seem to be that:

- If they share the accommodation with their landlord the landlord is liable, not them.

- Otherwise as a tenant or tenants they are liable rather than any sub-tenants or guests (licensees) who might be living with them.

However,

- If they are joint tenants they are jointly liable.

Also, even if they have individual tenancies, if they are all resident in the same house or flat they appear to be jointly liable for Council Tax purposes.

Any full-time student who has left their usual main residence to study elsewhere but retains owner occupier or tenant rights over it should have this property exempted from Council Tax liability as well.

Council Tax Benefit

As its name suggests, Council Tax Benefit (CTB) helps people on low incomes pay their Council Tax. The rules relating to eligibility for CTB are detailed and complex and, given that most students do not qualify, are only summarised here.

If you need more information on CTB the best source is *Guide to Housing Benefit and Council Tax Benefit* by John Zebedee and Martin Ward, published by Shelter and the Chartered Institute of Housing.

Normally, anyone who has to pay Council Tax and whose income does not exceed certain limits can get CTB, although there are some difficult cases, for example, 'persons from abroad'. As full-time students are not normally liable to pay Council Tax, the issue of claiming CTB does not arise. However, given that sometimes students are liable to pay (above) the question of whether they can claim CTB can be important.

Are students eligible for Council Tax Benefit?

Not normally. Full-time students are generally excluded from entitlement to CTB (see regulations 38-40 of the Council Tax Benefit (General) Regulations 1992). In general it is irrelevant whether they receive any kind of grant or other financial support. The exclusion even applies to full-time students not on higher education courses, unless they are under 19.

It can be difficult in some cases to decide whether a student is full-time or part-time. The rules have been changed recently, and there is some difficult case law (primarily in relation to eligibility for Income Support and Job Seeker's Allowance, where the same rule applies). At its simplest, someone is a full-time student if they are undertaking a full-time course of study. In the case of non-higher education courses, this generally means courses of more than 16 hours per week of guided study. In the case of higher education courses, it is necessary to examine the particular programme of study. There may be particular difficulty with modular courses which do not specify whether they are full-time or part-time.

If the college allows a student to interrupt their course temporarily because they are ill, or caring for someone else, they should not be regarded during this period as a full-time student.

Otherwise, once someone begins a full-time course of study they are treated as a student until the last day of the course (unless they abandon the course or are dismissed from it early). So, if a student simply interrupts their course for personal or academic reasons they are normally still deemed to be a student during this time even if they have little or no contact with the college and receive no financial help in their capacity as 'student'. Whether someone is a full-time or part-time student can be difficult to decide. If you are uncertain about your position, always seek advice.

The main categories of full-time students who can claim CTB are:

• lone parents

• students in a couple where their partner is not a full-time student or where they are responsible for a child or young person

• students aged 60 or more

• students who qualify for a disability premium

• students who have been incapable of work for 28 weeks or more.

In such cases it becomes necessary to calculate what CTB may be payable (again please note, the following should only be taken as an outline guide).

In general CTB is calculated by:

• Assessing the whole of a claimants' weekly eligible Council Tax

then

- Reducing this figure in line with the deductions laid down if there are any non-dependants living with the claimant. Non-dependants are usually adult children or other relatives or friends who live in the claimant's household on a non-commercial basis. The deductions represent the amount it is assumed such non-dependants will contribute towards the claimant's Council Tax, but they are implemented whether the person actually contributes or not. Situations where no deductions are made include those where the non-dependants are themselves on Income Support or Income-based Job Seeker's Allowance, or are under 18, or are themselves full-time students.

then, after the non-dependant deduction has been made

- Reducing CTB actually paid by 20% of income which is in excess of the minimum laid down by law for a person to live on (known as their 'applicable amount'). This figure is affected by whether the claimant is a lone parent, whether there are children, and if so how old they are, whether the claimant is disabled, and many other factors (for details see any of the specialist texts on benefits and welfare rights mentioned on page 144). There is also a capital limit of £16,000 and (for most claimants) capital between £3,000 and £6,000 produces an extra nominal 'tariff' income of £1 for every £250.

Non-dependent deductions can be difficult and complex. If you think you have a problem with them, or simply want to check details such as the precise figures involved, please consult one of the specialist books mentioned earlier or take advice.

Perhaps the trickiest issue to arise in relation to student eligibility for CTB concerns the treatment of student loans.

In calculating CTB all students eligible to apply for a student loan are assumed to be receiving one at the maximum level applicable to them. This applies irrespective of whether they actually receive a loan. Then, even though it is a loan, the whole amount is taken into account as income, less deductions for books and equipment and travel. The resulting figure is then averaged over the period from the first Monday in September to the last Sunday in June (42/43 weeks). From the resulting weekly figure, £10 per week is deducted. The remainder counts as income for CTB purposes.

This can cause problems. Not all students eligible for CTB will appreciate that their student loan can count as income. Please seek advice on this.

Housing Benefit

Even though most students do not pay Council Tax, nearly all of them pay rent or some equivalent payment for residential rights over the property they live in. Unfortunately, most students do not qualify for Housing Benefit (HB) to assist with the cost of this. Much of what has been said in relation to CTB also applies here:

- full-time students on higher education courses are generally not eligible for HB (Regulation 48 A(1) of the Housing Benefit (General) Regulations 1987 treats such a person as if they were 'not liable to make payments in respect of a dwelling')

- a number of groups of students are exempt from this, the rules being very much the same as for CTB (see above)

- student loans count as 'income'

- non-dependant deductions are made.

The main differences between the HB and CTB calculations are:

If you live in a hall of residence or any other accommodation where your college/university is your landlord (see chapter 7) you are not eligible for HB even if you are a part-time student or part of a couple where your partner is not a student. This special rule only applies during term time.

You may not be eligible (even if you otherwise qualify for HB) on term time accommodation if it is vacated during the summer. There are numerous exceptions to this. Please seek advice.

The income 'taper' for HB purpose is 65% rather than 20%.

Before assuming that all your rent will be covered by HB if you do qualify for it, please seek advice on issues such as the relevance of any non-dependants you may have living with you (see above) and how student loans are treated.

Case

Jan was a single mother with a young child. She was a part time student at a college in the Midlands who rented a housing association property on an assured tenancy.

She contacted Shelter when her landlord took possession proceedings for rent arrears. She had been in receipt of income support since her tenancy started four months ago and should have been receiving full housing benefit (HB) but the claim had not been processed.

Initially Shelter helped her to get the court proceedings adjourned for 28 days on the basis that her HB claim was outstanding. However two months later the landlord advised that they were returning to court to seek a possession order, as the HB had not been paid.

The case was once again adjourned and the judge asked for a witness summons to be issued to the Housing Benefit Section.

Shelter contacted the Housing Benefit Section on Jan's behalf to advise them that a witness summons was going to be issued if the claim was not processed straightaway. The HB was subsequently processed, the arrears cleared and the possession order action halted.

Shelter also advised Jan to seek compensation for the distress and inconvenience caused by the HB delays, which had had a detrimental effect on her college work. This involved issuing a complaint to the Housing Benefit Section followed by a referral to the Local Government Ombudsman.

Jan and her son were able to stay in her home and the Housing Benefit Section eventually agreed to pay her compensation.

Subjects covered in this chapter include...

Safety issues

The landlord's responsibility for repairs

The tenant's obligations

What can be done about disrepair

Taking legal action

Compensation

Inevitably, most students have to rent accommodation at the cheaper end of the market. It is almost equally inevitable that they will encounter problems with the condition of their accommodation. Even in some college accommodation, they may face problems and have to cope with older or cheaper furniture and equipment.

Unfortunately, as Jan Luba, a well known housing lawyer, points out:

> **'Our repairs law is a messy, overlapping conglomeration of rules, rights, powers and duties derived from a host of statutes, cases and regulations.'**

However, there is no reason why students should have to live in unsafe or insanitary accommodation and some providers of student accommodation do make substantial efforts to ensure good standards by imposing a code of standards on participating landlords.

There are also important laws and regulations that relate to these issues. In the case of gas supply and fittings, it is a criminal offence for a landlord to rent out accommodation without a current safety certificate. Other provisions cover electricity and fire safety.

In practice, the best time to attempt to resolve difficulties about disrepair and safety is before signing the tenancy agreement.

After the tenancy has begun, the written agreement (if any) provides the starting point for resolving these problems.

Standard letting agreements usually indicate that the landlord is responsible for maintaining the main fabric of the premises, and the fixed installations to do with water, gas, electricity and sanitation. However, in most cases the law imposes these obligations on landlords whether this is mentioned in the tenancy agreement or not, or even if there is no written tenancy agreement at all.

The situation regarding responsibility for the state of decoration and supplied equipment can be more difficult to resolve, as agreements may say nothing about them other than indicating that the occupier must not damage them.

Having established who is responsible, the next major hurdle is trying to get the landlord to carry out their obligations. While this can be difficult in practice, ultimately students can sue landlords in the county court to make them carry out work or pay compensation.

The local authority's environmental health service may be able to help. In some situations involving poor housing conditions, they have an obligation to act against bad landlords. In other situations, while they have the power to act, they are not obliged to.

Safety issues

There is a patchwork of statutory requirements that relate to safety issues. In parts of the country where the amount of private rented accommodation available exceeds demand, many colleges have successfully established accreditation schemes. These require landlords to provide safety certificates as a prerequisite to letting through the university or college accommodation service. It is more difficult for colleges to impose a system like this in areas where demand exceeds supply.

Gas

Deaths and serious injuries have been caused by carbon monoxide seeping out of old or unserviced gas appliances. It is essential that the fumes from gas boilers, water heaters and fires leave the accommodation via a chimney or piping (flue). Chimneys and flues must be kept unblocked and fully enclosed. Under the Gas Safety Regulations 1998, all landlords are responsible for ensuring that gas appliances and flues are

- maintained in good order

  and

- checked for safety at least every 12 months by a CORGI registered gas installer.

Landlords are obliged to keep a record of the safety checks and supply them to existing occupiers within 28 days of the check being carried out. Prospective occupiers must be given a copy of the latest check before moving in. If you have concerns about this, you should contact your local environmental health department. Further information can also be obtained from the Gas Safety Advice Line: 0800 300 363.

Electricity

Landlords have a general responsibility for the electricity supply in your accommodation and for any electrical appliances they provide. If you believe they are not safe, you should notify the landlord in writing. There are currently no national safety standards for electrical installations, though in May 2002 the Government announced proposals to review the need for them. In practice, many university or college accommodation services require private landlords to have certificates of electrical safety issued by the NICEIC (National Inspection Council for Electrical Installation Contracting) or ECA (Electrical Contractors Association).

Fire: means of escape

Your accommodation should have a clear, safe and uncluttered exit route in case of fire. In terms of the law, environmental health officers have some obligations to ensure that there are adequate means of escape from fire but only where the accommodation is regarded as a 'house in multiple occupation' (HMO).

Houses occupied by students and divided into self-contained flats or bedsits would be regarded as HMOs. However, where students rent a whole house as a group, the law does not currently regard the arrangement as capable of being an HMO. For more information, see the section on HMOs on page 78.

Given that HMOs are regarded as the least safe type of housing, landlords may be required to provide lobbies and fire-check doors and/or doors with self-closing devices along escape routes. University or college accommodation services may require private landlords to make such provisions under their college landlord accreditation scheme.

Fire precautions

Fire precautions usually only include the provision of smoke detectors, fire extinguishers and fire blankets in HMOs. There is no statutory requirement for other accommodation. However, as a bare minimum, students should acquire their own smoke detectors. The fitting of smoke detectors is often required as part of a university or college landlord accreditation scheme.

Furnishings and furniture

All furnishings and furniture in rented accommodation must be made of materials that have passed specified ignitability tests. This covers all kinds of seating, beds and bedding. All furniture produced since 1988 must be labelled with an indication that it complies with the Furniture and Furnishings (Fire Safety) Regulations 1988. To pursue the matter, you should contact your local trading standards office. You should bear in mind that they have the power to remove unsafe items.

What is the landlord responsible for?

At a bare minimum, the landlord is responsible for those items mentioned in a written agreement. This forms a contract between you and the landlord. Breaking its terms can lead to you being entitled to compensation from the landlord for the misery of living in poor conditions and any additional costs you have incurred as a consequence, for example, additional heating costs where accommodation is damp. In the most serious cases, it would also justify you leaving and cancelling a fixed period letting early, but you need to take advice in these circumstances.

What are the tenant's obligations?

The law does impose some basic obligations on tenants. They are not responsible for repairing items damaged through general wear and tear but they must not deliberately damage the property. They are also obliged to behave in a 'tenant-like' manner. This means doing 'the little jobs about the place which a reasonable tenant would do', for example, getting blocked sinks unblocked, fixing the lights when they fuse, and turning off water if they go away for a substantial period of time.

Case

A group of students went away for the Christmas vacation but did not leave the central heating on for a few hours each day, despite a specific clause in the agreement requiring them to do so. When they returned in January, pipes had burst, the property was completely flooded and all the ceilings had collapsed, rendering it uninhabitable. The students had to find temporary rooms with friends.

The landlord indicated he would carry out repairs as quickly as possible and the students moved back in after two months. It was agreed that no rent would be charged for this period and that the landlord would recover the cost of the damage from the students' deposits at the end of the tenancy.

Where a tenant wants to pursue a compensation claim against a landlord because of disrepair, the claim could be reduced where the tenant has failed to

- minimise damage caused by a disrepair by not promptly reporting problems to the landlord

  and

- where possible, stop damage spreading. Where, for example, a ceiling is leaking, tenants should try and catch the drips in a bucket.

While landlords are responsible for repairs, they are not obliged to do things that amount to improvements. This usually means that you cannot demand the installation of central heating if none was there when you moved in. However, if the central heating is broken or malfunctioning, the landlord is obliged to ensure that it works properly.

One of the most problematic issues is dampness. Dampness can be caused by condensation, construction processes or it can be rising or penetrating damp (see table below). Frequently condensation is not regarded as falling within the definition of disrepair. Often the fabric of the building is not in a state of disrepair and its cure involves making substantial improvements. However, it is very likely to constitute a statutory nuisance and action can be taken by the local authority's environmental health service.

Identifying the problem: dampness

Possible characteristics	Damp patches on walls, damp smell in newly built or renovated property.	Bands of dampness and discoloration on ground floor walls up to a height of 18"- 36". Damp and/or rotten floor boards.	Patches of damp and/or mould, for example, in a corner of the ceiling, underneath the windowsill or on the walls. Crumbling plaster.	Condensation on windows, puddles gathering on windowsills. Mould and dampness, or even drops of water, all over (usually) an outside wall. Can affect bedclothes near that wall or the contents of cupboards.
Type of dampness	Construction processes	Rising damp	Penetrating damp	Condensation
Cause	Plaster or concrete slabs not properly dried out.	Defective or absent damp proof course (DPC). Water logging of the surrounding ground due to inadequate drainage.	Faulty construction or lack of maintenance. Windows and doors that don't fit, holes in the roof, old or inadequate pointing to the brickwork, faulty joints in concrete slabs, blocked or leaking gutters, etc.	Warm moist air meets cooler wall surface or windows. Inadequate ventilation, insulation, heating and or poor building design.
Remedy	Drying out.	Repair or insertion of DPC.	Repair fault, replastering.	Increase insulation, ventilation and/or heating.

Tenancies

Where you have a tenancy of any kind, the law imposes basic repairing obligations on landlords of residential property under section 11 of the Landlord and Tenant Act 1985. These apply to assured, assured shorthold, non assured, non assured college lets, council accommodation and even excluded tenancies. They apply irrespective of what the tenancy agreement says or even of the existence of a written tenancy agreement. However, the obligation to repair only arises once the landlord has been notified or has become aware of the disrepair. It follows that tenants should report items of disrepair to the landlord as soon as possible.

These obligations can only be excluded in very limited circumstances i.e. where

- the tenancy started before 24 October 1961, or

- there is a lease for seven years or more, or

- the parties agreed and obtained a court order authorising them to contract out.

The landlord is obliged to keep in repair the structure and exterior of the dwelling house. This includes drains, gutters and external pipes.

They are also obliged to keep in repair and proper working order the installations in the dwelling house for the supply of

- water

- gas

- electricity

- sanitation

- space heating, and

- hot water.

This includes basins, sinks, baths and toilets but not other fixtures, fittings and appliances that make use of the water, gas and electricity supplies, for example, a cooker or fridge.

These obligations extend to the shared common parts of a building, for example hallways and lifts, if the tenancy started after 15 January 1989.

Defective premises

Section 4 of the Defective Premises Act 1972 makes landlords liable to tenants for injuries caused by the landlords' failure to keep the premises in a safe state of repair. This will be the case provided the landlord is responsible for repairs (see above). This does not get repairs done but can give the tenant compensation if an injury results from a failure to carry them out. Landlords are liable if they knew or ought to have known of the defect that caused the injury. It is thus not always necessary for tenants to prove that they notified the landlord of the defect before the injury was caused.

Licences

Neither section 11 of the Landlord & Tenant Act 1985 nor the Defective Premises Act 1972 (see above) applies where occupiers only have a licence. However, environmental health provisions (see below) can apply, as they do not differentiate between licences and tenancies.

What can be done about disrepair?

In the first case, the most important thing to do is to make a formal request in writing for the work to be done (and keep a copy). Set out what needs attention and give the landlord a reasonable period to do the work. How long this is will depend on

- how much work is required, and

- how seriously the disrepair is impacting on you.

Many colleges, local authorities, registered social landlords and reputable private companies have scheduled repair periods for different types of repair, for example, 48 hours for emergency works, one to two weeks for essential works, etc.

Where you feel the landlord fails to respond adequately, you could seek assistance from the university or college accommodation service, a Citizens Advice Bureau, a Shelter Housing Aid Centre or a solicitor. Law schools in some universities operate free advice services run by supervised law students. They may be able to negotiate successfully on your behalf to get the repairs done.

Some local authorities run arbitration or mediation schemes that may be able to resolve the problem.

In practice, most disrepair cases are resolved through negotiation, but if this does not work there are four possible courses of action to consider:

- Give up the accommodation.

- Get the repairs done yourself and claim the money back from the landlord.

- Take legal action against the landlord.

- Get the local authority's Environmental Health Service involved.

After you have read about these options, please read the section on disrepair strategies on page 79. This should help you to decide what to do.

Giving up the accommodation

If it is near the end of term, you may grit your teeth and put up with it until you leave. If there is other (better) accommodation available, you might want to leave. In that case, you will have to follow the guidelines in chapter 8 ('I want to leave'). You should get legal advice where you want to leave before a fixed term agreement has expired. If you do, remember to let the university or college accommodation service know about the problem so that they can remove the accommodation from their lists or, at least, tip off potential future tenants.

Getting the repairs done yourself

Since the 1971 court decision in *Lee-Parker v. Izzett,* it has been possible for tenants to get repairs done where landlords would not do them. This is on the basis that the tenant pays for the repairs and then deducts the cost from the rent payments.

The procedure

Tenants need to follow carefully the guidelines set out in the case. This means the tenant should

- Inform the landlord in writing of the repairs needed and ask for them to be done.

- Allow the landlord a reasonable period of time to get the work done.

- If the work is not done, the tenant should get at least three estimates for the cost of the work. Send copies to the landlord with a letter giving a further time limit for the work to be done, failing which the tenant will get the work done.

- If the landlord still fails to carry out the work, the tenant can instruct the person who submitted the lowest estimate to do the work.

- After the work has been completed, the tenant pays the bill. Make sure you get receipts for work done and materials bought.

- Send a copy of the bill and proof of payment to the landlord to pay. It is best to use recorded delivery.

- If the landlord does not reimburse the tenant, the tenant can deduct the cost from future rent payments. The tenant must restart paying rent to the landlord once the bill has been recovered.

Issues to bear in mind before you start

- You must be sure that these particular repairs are the landlord's responsibility.

- Remember that this will not cover improvements.

- This will only work if you can afford to pay the bill for the repairs once they have been completed.

- If the bill is high, this is committing you to staying for some time to recover your money.

- You will technically be in rent arrears and the landlord may respond by trying to evict you. You need to be aware of your housing status. If, for example, you are an assured shorthold tenant staying on after a fixed term agreement ended, the landlord may seek to evict you simply by giving eight weeks notice rather than on the basis of rent arrears. See chapter 8 for full details.

- The cost is deductible from future rent payments, not rent arrears. You cannot withhold rent to save up for the repairs. However, if rent arrears have accrued and a landlord takes court action claiming those arrears, it may be possible to ask the court to offset the arrears against the costs of the repairs. Provided the repair costs exceed the rent arrears, this could cancel out the claim. This is an issue where you should get legal advice before defending the legal action.

- The tenant is responsible for the work carried out. If it is done poorly or negligently, the tenant is responsible.

- It is crucial to keep copies of all the letters, estimates, etc.

Taking legal action

It is essential to seek legal advice before starting court proceedings. The law recognises the difficulties in taking legal action on disrepair by having a different threshold for small claims in the county court than for other cases. If a disrepair claim is for less than £1,000, it is dealt with as a small claim. This means that a tenant does not normally have to pay the other side's legal costs even if they lose the case. Of course, it also means that you cannot recover legal costs if you win the case. Where a disrepair claim is for more than £1,000, however, it may be dealt with as a mainstream case by the county court. This means that claimants may be eligible for legal aid to employ a solicitor for these cases.

Where legal action is based on a landlord's failure to comply with their contractual obligations, it is important to have

- written evidence of when you complained to the landlord about the problems, and
- evidence of the amount of money you have spent to back up a damages claim.

The courts can make orders for

- specific performance – an order to the landlord to carry out repairs, and
- damages – payment from the landlord to compensate for the losses you have suffered as a result of the landlord's failure to carry out the repairs.

Damages can cover payment for things like

- physical discomfort suffered
- inconvenience caused
- not being able to use part of the accommodation
- the cost of alternative accommodation if the conditions were so bad you were forced to move out
- the costs of redecoration or cleaning up
- damage or injury to your health
- works you had to carry out
- damage to your belongings
- the costs of purchasing heaters where the landlord failed to repair existing heaters.

Launching a counter claim

When a landlord takes legal proceedings against a tenant, the tenant may be able to counter-claim successfully if the landlord has failed to maintain the accommodation properly. This is most likely to arise if the landlord is making a money claim, for example, for rent arrears. Compensation awarded to the tenant can be offset against the landlord's claim.

The Environmental Health Service (EHS)

All local authorities have environmental health departments, though their titles may vary slightly. The authorities have a wide variety of statutory duties and powers which relate to housing. They are under a duty to take some action to improve your living conditions if your accommodation constitutes a 'statutory nuisance' or is 'unfit for human habitation'. They may take a number of courses of action to deal with your problems in other situations or if you are in a 'house in multiple occupation'. Where the EHS has discretion about taking action, it often shows a marked reluctance to act because of the cost to the council.

Statutory nuisance

Premises are a statutory nuisance where they are in such a state that they are 'prejudicial to health or a nuisance'. Prejudicial to health is defined as injurious or 'likely to cause injury' to health. The concept has recently been described in court as applying to filthy or unwholesome premises likely to cause disease or illness.

The following are likely to be statutory nuisances:

- blocked drains or toilets

- leaking roof

- loose banisters

- piles of rubbish

- dangerous wiring

- broken lavatory

- serious dampness

- dangerous structures.

A defect could be a statutory nuisance if it could be a danger or nuisance to neighbours or passers-by, for example:

- serious damp coming in from next door

- tiles falling from roof into the street

- rotten window frames which might fall out.

Complaints made about poor housing conditions must be investigated by the EHS where they constitute a statutory nuisance under the Environmental Protection Act 1990. Where the EHS is satisfied that a statutory nuisance exists, it must serve an abatement notice. This requires the landlord to end or remove the nuisance within a specified time. Non-compliance with the notice is a criminal offence and the EHS can prosecute the landlord in the local magistrates court. It can also undertake works in default and recover the cost from the landlord. Where a defect is structural, notice must be served on the owner of the property.

There is a right of appeal to the magistrates court against an abatement notice (within 21 days of service). The Secretary of State for the Environment has made regulations about the circumstances in which notices may be suspended pending appeal and specifying grounds for appeal.

It is possible for tenants to prosecute landlords, though you are only likely to consider this where the EHS refuses to act or your landlord is the local authority itself. You need legal advice before doing this.

Magistrates court hearings for statutory nuisance

If the magistrates are satisfied that a nuisance existed at the date the legal proceedings started, the person taking the action is automatically entitled to costs (expenses) even if the nuisance was ended or abated before the court hearing. If they are satisfied that a statutory nuisance still exists, they must make a nuisance order requiring abatement and may impose a fine. If a nuisance is 'likely to recur', the court can make an order to carry out repairs to prevent a recurrence.

Compensation

Under the Powers of Criminal Courts Act 1973, the magistrates court can make a compensation order for 'any personal injury, loss or damage' resulting from the offence up to a maximum of £5,000. While the courts have said that compensation orders are appropriate especially where a civil court could not award damages, i.e. because there was no disrepair liability, they have also said that

- substantial awards should not be made where they can be recovered in civil proceedings (especially for personal injury),

   and that

- compensation should be calculated from the date the notice was issued to the date of conviction. In other words, it does not cover the whole period of the nuisance.

Fitness for human habitation

As you might expect, accommodation must be fit for human habitation. If it is not, the EHS must act. An extensive legal definition sets out a basic standard all accommodation must meet. Factors that can lead to accommodation being deemed unfit include:

- serious disrepair
- stability problems with the accommodation
- dampness which is prejudicial to the occupiers' health
- inadequate natural lighting
- inadequate ventilation
- poor or non-existent water supply
- inadequate facilities for the preparation and cooking of food
- inadequate drainage or toilet facilities.

While the EHS must take some action, it can choose from a wide range of options. According to the law, it must take 'the most satisfactory course of action' taking into account detailed guidance provided by the Department of the Environment. This could include:

- issuing a repair notice to the landlord requiring the carrying out of specified work

- requiring the property to be demolished (a demolition order)

- ordering that nobody be allowed to live there (a closing order).

In the latter two cases, you are entitled to be rehoused by the local authority.

Often student housing will not be bad enough to be classed as a statutory nuisance, but failure to carry out essential repairs to deal with dampness or bad plumbing could render a property unfit for human habitation. It may be worth complaining to the local authority to see if it will serve a repair notice to make the landlord deal with the problem.

Case

Ten students moved into a large house. They approached their university Accommodation Office after receiving an electric shock from a wall plug, and noticing sewage leaking into the back yard from a soil pipe, with the result that only one of three WCs was usable. The local authority Environmental Health Department was contacted. They immediately declared the house unfit for human habitation, and served a seven-day Repair Notice for the plumbing, electrical and other defects they found. After seven days the repairs had not been carried out, and the students were advised to find other accommodation. They were reluctant to do so as ten bedroom properties were rare and it meant the group would have to split up.

After further inactivity by the landlord, the local authority started proceedings and eventually the students realised they had to move out. The works were done by the local authority in default, and they persuaded the landlord to split the house into smaller flats. The landlord's properties were also removed from the local accreditation scheme, and the students consulted a solicitor, who was successful in obtaining compensation.

Houses in Multiple Occupation (HMOs)

The law gives local authorities certain powers to take action to deal with poor housing conditions for property that comes within the definition of a 'house in multiple occupation' (HMO). An HMO is a house which is occupied by people who are not a single household.

Where a property is an HMO, the EHO has a wide range of powers to deal with poor housing conditions. These can cover ending overcrowding and requiring the installation of sufficient and adequate living facilities. These could relate to:

• cooking facilities

• sinks

• toilets

• wash basins

• baths or showers

• hot and cold water

• adequate means of escape from fire

• other adequate fire precautions.

The definition of HMO covers houses that have been let out as bed-sits or which contain self-contained flats. It also covers purpose built accommodation such as halls of residence. While many students share rented houses with other students, they usually live independent lives to varying degrees. Unfortunately, it seems clear at present that most shared student houses are not regarded as HMOs. This follows a Court of Appeal decision made in 1995 *(Barnes v. Sheffield CC)*.

The test for deciding whether a house is an HMO or not is multi-faceted. It was decided in the Barnes case that the following factors have to be taken into account:

• The origins of the tenancy. Where students arrive as a group this suggests a single household.

• Whether facilities are shared. The greater the degree of sharing, the greater the likelihood of a single household.

• Whether the occupiers are responsible for the whole house or only individual rooms. Shared responsibility for the whole suggests a single household.

• Door locks. Their absence on individuals' rooms suggests a single household.

- Who is responsible for filling vacancies? If it is the group, this is suggestive of a single household.

- How rooms are allocated. If it is by the group rather than the landlord, this is suggestive of a single household.

- Number of occupiers. The larger the number, the less likelihood there is of them constituting a single household.

- Stability of the group. The more frequently occupiers come and go, the less likelihood there is of them constituting a single household.

- Mode of living. Greater degrees of communal living suggest a single household.

Disrepair strategies

You do not have to choose either to take legal action against the landlord or to get the environmental health involved – you could do both. However, you need to be aware of what each can achieve and the relative advantages and disadvantages.

The advantages of the local authority taking environmental health action can include:

- You may be able to persuade the landlord that it isn't you who is 'causing trouble'.

- The local authority takes responsibility for the legal action.

- It doesn't cost the tenant anything.

- It can get some problems dealt with that are not strictly covered by disrepair obligations, for example, condensation.

The disadvantages may be:

- The standard of repair required may be just enough to deal with the problem i.e. 'a patch' which has not resolved it in the long term.

- The amount of compensation you get is likely to be very limited.

- You have no control over how the matter is resolved.

- The whole process is much more complicated if the local authority is the landlord.

- It can still take months.

The advantages of taking legal action yourself based on your landlord's breach of the contract can include:

- You initiate and have control over the action.
- You can claim compensation from the landlord to cover most of the losses you have suffered.
- Legal aid may be available to pay for a lawyer if your claim is for more than £1,000.

The disadvantages may be:

- The definition of repair doesn't cover all poor housing conditions.
- You must be able to show that you gave the landlord notice that repairs were needed (though this need not be the case if your claim is based on the Defective Premises Act).
- It may take quite some time to resolve.
- You will need to pay a lawyer if you are not eligible for legal aid.

Subjects covered in this chapter include...

Who is a neighbour

Problems with noise

Actions that can be taken

Problems other than noise

Unreasonable behaviour and eviction

Liability for other people's behaviour

Noise and disturbance from those living next door, or a generally bad and difficult atmosphere with co-occupiers, can be just as large an issue as the property itself being in a bad state or having problems with the landlord. Much of the law about neighbours is far from clear-cut so legal solutions (even where theoretically available) may well make neighbour problems worse. This chapter therefore looks at the law and legal remedies but also considers a range of 'non legal' approaches that might help.

'Who then in law is my neighbour?'

This question is taken from the judgment of Lord Atkin in *Donoghue v. Stevenson* 1932. In it, Lord Atkin uses the concept of 'neighbour' as the basis of establishing liability in the law of negligence. In effect he states that everyone owes a duty to be careful to his or her 'neighbours'. He answers his own question by saying that your 'neighbour' is someone likely to be 'closely and directly' affected by your conduct. In the housing context with which we are concerned, the law has generally used the word 'neighbour' in a more restrictive sense – generally those who live next door or (at least) nearby. However, Lord Atkin's wider use of the term may have relevance when considering relationships between occupiers in the same house or flat and, in particular, the responsibility a landlord might have concerning the behaviour of occupants of their properties.

In cases of noise or other disturbances a 'neighbour' is generally the person occupying 'neighbouring' premises. This need not necessarily be the person immediately next door but in practice is likely to be someone living fairly close, as you need to be badly affected by the noise or other disturbance to have significant rights.

If the problem relates to harassment or intimidation, you may have rights against the perpetrator whether they live in the same property as you, next door, nearby, or completely outside the locality. If you believe that you are in danger of physical violence you should contact the police. However, the ways in which you can legally protect yourself or seek compensation may depend on where the perpetrator lives.

If the complaint is against you, and you are being threatened with possible eviction as a result, you may have a problem if your conduct or that of anyone living with or even visiting you caused actual (or potential) nuisance or annoyance to anyone in the locality. Locality is not precisely defined in law but seems to mean the neighbourhood or area.

I can't sleep because of the noise

Noise is one of the most common complaints and sources of friction. People have greatly differing sensitivities to 'noise pollution' and this is not as is sometimes supposed simply a matter of age. The rap music fan living in the room next to you in hall, or the heavy metal aficionado living in the house next door, may fail to appreciate that their enjoyment of music played at maximum volume is not matched by yours! The problem of noisy neighbours, like much of this chapter, raises issues not only of what the law is but also whether the use of legal sanctions is the most satisfactory way of dealing with things.

What is the law?

The control of excessive noise is mainly through two separate areas of law – the common law tort of private nuisance and the 'public' controls imposed by the Environmental Protection Act 1990 and the Noise Act 1996.

A tort is what lawyers call a civil wrong, in other words it is not a criminal matter involving the police but something which has to be resolved between those affected. Private nuisance is usually defined as any unlawful interference with another's use or enjoyment of their property. A nuisance can be caused by unpleasant smells, smoke, the escape of water, blocking off someone's light, and even in one case an 'offensive' sex shop.

Noise nuisance is, however, the commonest example. At the heart of the tort is the idea that the person responsible for the smoke, smells or noise had been behaving unreasonably. We all need to put up with some irritations – particularly if we live in cities. No-one has a right to absolute peace and quiet or freedom from disturbance by others. As long ago as 1862 a court said that it was all a matter of 'give and take, of live and let live' (*Bamford v. Turnley*). Unfortunately, therefore, there is no simple test for deciding whether the noise caused by your neighbour is excessive. Of course there will be obvious cases – for example, music played at high volume repeatedly throughout the night – but in most cases there is scope for argument.

It is also possible for noise to be so widespread in an area that it amounts to what is called a public nuisance, which is a criminal offence (an example might be an outdoor music festival). If that seems a possibility, seek legal advice, preferably in conjunction with others affected.

The Environmental Protection Act 1990 section 79 (1)(g) says that noise 'emitted from premises so as to be prejudicial to health or a nuisance' amounts to a statutory nuisance. No particular formula is specified by the legislation – on receiving a complaint about noise a council has to use its own professional judgment about whether the level and repetition of the noise is excessive. So, although complaining to the council and having it check noise levels may make sense, there is no guarantee that it will take the same view as you about how 'excessive' the noise is.

Night-time noise is often the real issue and here the Noise Act 1996 may apply. If it receives a complaint about excessive noise between 11pm and 7am, a council has to take 'reasonable steps' to investigate the complaint. Under the legislation the noise will be 'excessive' if it exceeds permitted levels (which may be varied from time to time) as measured by an employee of the council. If you are concerned about noise levels, it is worthwhile having the level checked by the council to see if it exceeds the maximum level permitted.

So what steps can I take?

Again the approach differs, depending whether the issue is private nuisance, or whether the Noise and Environmental Protection Acts apply.

You may be able to resolve the problem yourself by talking to your neighbour, who may not appreciate that their behaviour is causing a problem.

If your attempts at amicable resolution fail, however, the most common approach concerning private nuisance is to send a 'legal letter' to try to induce the offender to moderate their activities. Such a letter would most typically come from a solicitor but a similar effect might be obtained by a letter from the Students' Union Welfare Service or other advice agency (see chapter 9). Of course 'threatening' letters might simply make matters worse!

If all else fails, you can try to obtain an injunction against your neighbour. An injunction is a court order which prohibits an activity or places curbs upon it. So, it could prohibit the creation of noise at specified times, and/or place specified limits on noise levels (for an example of this see *Kennaway v. Thompson* 1980 in which the Court of Appeal granted an injunction to the owner of a house near a lake on which power boat racing was held which limited the use of the lake to certain days and to certain noise limits). However, all this could take a long time, could be expensive (legal aid may not be available), and is not certain of success, particularly given the lack of precision about what level of noise is so unreasonable as to amount to a private nuisance.

Under the Environmental Protection Act 1990 the likeliest response of the council will be to send out one of its specialist 'noise officers' to check the level of noise on a number of occasions. If, as a result, it takes the view that the noise is 'excessive' and that, therefore, a statutory nuisance exists, it is under a duty to issue an abatement notice requiring the noise level to be reduced. If your neighbour continues to make the noise despite the notice they are guilty of an offence.

Under the Noise Act 1996, once a council has received a complaint about night-time noise it has to take 'reasonable steps' to investigate the complaint (most likely in the same way as under the Environmental Protection Act). If the noise exceeds the specified level the council has the power to issue a warning notice. If your neighbour continues to make excessive noise after receiving such a notice they are guilty of an offence. The receipt of a warning notice, like an abatement notice, can, in itself, be a fairly effective deterrent. If you feel that trying to settle the issue with your neighbour amicably won't work there is much to be said for contacting the council immediately rather than getting caught up in all the uncertainty of a private nuisance dispute.

Actually it's my flat-mates who are the real problem

Legally, as well as practically, this is a real problem! All of the law discussed above presupposes that the noise comes from neighbouring premises. Certainly a private nuisance, whether based on noise or any other disturbance, only exists if it comes from another building or another piece of land. The most recent case law on what is now the Environmental Health Act 1990 (*National Coal Board v. Neath Borough Council* 1976) makes it clear that a 'statutory nuisance' must be either a private or public nuisance or 'prejudicial to health' (not just personal comfort!). So the Environmental Health Act only applies if the noise is coming from neighbouring premises, unless it is so distressing that it is affecting your health. Finally, the Noise Act 1996 is explicit that the noise has to come from 'another dwelling' (s.2 1996 Act).

So, what can you do if your flat-mates (whether joint tenants or not) disturb you with their noisy nocturnal activities? A practical approach may be called for – either trying to talk things through with them or, if this fails, complaining to your landlord. The extent to which a landlord is legally compelled to act in such a case is discussed next.

Is it worth complaining to the landlord?

Of course, the next door neighbour responsible for the noise or other disturbance may be an owner occupier. If, however, they rent the property you may feel that 'justice' suggests that their landlord should have some legal responsibility for what is happening. Unfortunately the law is not particularly encouraging about the extent of a landlord's responsibility.

So, what is the law?

Generally, the person liable in private nuisance is the person in possession of the premises, which normally means the tenant and not the landlord. This was confirmed in *Smith v. Scott* 1973 where the claimants had to move out of their house because the problem family next door had made their life intolerable by noise and vandalism.

However,

- If those responsible for the nuisance are not tenants but only licensees or trespassers, possession of the premises is, in law, retained by the landlord. If a landlord lets such people into possession, knowing of their tendencies, or fails to take steps to control them while they are there, they may themselves be liable in nuisance (*Lippiatt v. South Gloucestershire Council* 1999).

- In extreme cases it might be possible to take action against a landlord in negligence, rather than in nuisance. A claim in negligence was also rejected in *Smith v. Scott,* on the basis that there was no general duty to take care to choose tenants who would not cause harm to their neighbours. This aspect of the case has been followed recently in *Hussain v. Lancaster City Council* and in *Mowan v. Wandsworth LBC.* All these cases involved councils with public housing duties and the courts clearly felt it would be an unreasonable extra burden upon them to impose a duty of care towards neighbours. It is arguable whether the same concerns should apply to private landlords, particularly where they knew or suspected that incoming tenants were potential troublemakers.

  Nevertheless, you must be aware that case law is against a landlord being liable.

- A landlord can be liable if they have 'explicitly authorised' the nuisance – that is, they have 'given the nod' to the activity while being aware of its nuisance-making potential. In *Smith v. Scott* this principle was not applied, in part because the council had inserted a clause into the relevant tenancy agreement forbidding the tenants to create a nuisance. So they could not be said to have 'authorised' the subsequent conduct of the tenants – if anything, the reverse.

So, again, the law is not encouraging about actions against landlords – particularly as a significant factor could be the existence of a 'no nuisance' clause in the tenancy agreement (which you will not have an automatic legal right to get access to).

Does it make a difference if the disturbances are being caused by my flat-mates?

As noted above, taking action against your flat-mates for noise and other disturbance is legally very difficult. It might, however, be worth complaining to your landlord. If you are in a joint tenant relationship with those causing the problem, or they are (in some way) part of your 'household', this could be a risky step since you may be liable yourself for what they do (this is discussed further below).

However, in other cases your landlord may be able to bring pressure to bear individually on the other(s) – in extreme cases by threatening, or actually taking, possession proceedings against them. Equally, there seems no way legally to force your landlord to act in this way.

What if I live in a hall of residence or other college or university owned or operated accommodation?

If you occupy a room in any kind of hall of residence then it is likely that your fellow residents in hall – like yourself – will have signed an agreement linking occupation of the hall to the university/college's general disciplinary regulations (for a full discussion of this, see chapter 7). These regulations will probably contain specific sanctions concerning misbehaviour in hall, ranging from fines to suspension or expulsion from university. Obviously this should concern you greatly if you are accused of such misbehaviour, but if you are a victim of it, complaining to the hall manager, warden or 'resident tutor' and ultimately the university accommodation service is likely to prove effective. Universities are acutely sensitive to discipline problems in halls – particularly as, to some extent, first year students in particular may be seen by their parents as under the 'care' of the college or university, even if the student is over 18 and this is not legally the case. Links to disciplinary regulations may also be found in 'head tenancy' and similar agreements (see, again, chapter 7) – but this is more variable in practice.

If your university landlord proves reluctant to act, it may be possible to put pressure on them via your department, or the students' union. Legally, the position of the university landlord seems much the same as other landlords and it is likely that the courts would be as reluctant to have extra burdens placed upon them to curb troublemakers or face legal liability as in the public landlord cases already mentioned.

> ## Case
>
> Complaints were made to the Hall Manager about Emma's boyfriend, Ken. He was staying with Emma frequently. He was unpleasant and aggressive towards the other students living on that floor and they suspected that he was stealing their food from the fridge. It was also rumoured that Ken was wanted by the police.
>
> After two informal warnings by the Hall Manager, Emma was called to a formal disciplinary hearing as she was in breach of her licence agreement by having a semi permanent guest. Ken had by this time been arrested and Emma was in financial trouble. Emma had made peace with the other students on the corridor. Emma was given a final written warning for breach of House Rules which formed part of the tenancy agreement.
>
> **Comment**
>
> This case emphasises the point that students need to be particularly aware that they can be held responsible for the behaviour of their guests.

What if the problem is something other than noise?

The law of private nuisance, with all its difficulties of enforcement, applies to a much wider range of activities than merely disturbance caused by noise. Examples of the wide range of 'unreasonable' activities seen to be nuisances include:

- allowing trees to overhang a neighbour's garden, or tree roots to penetrate the neighbour's property

- allowing a drain to become blocked so that the water flows onto a neighbour's land

- allowing offensive smells or smoke (for example from a factory) to drift over a neighbour's land

- allowing excessive heat to pass into a neighbour's property (in one case heat from kitchen stoves made a wine cellar unfit for its purpose!).

However, as already explained in relation to noise, there must be a lot of 'give and take' in urban society. A right to take action in nuisance does not arise merely because you dislike the smell of your neighbour's cooking.

Alternatively, the Environmental Protection Act 1990 section 79 also covers a much wider range of 'statutory nuisances' than merely noise nuisance. Specific instances are:

- 'smoke emitted from premises so as to be prejudicial to health or a nuisance' (s.79(1)(b))

- 'fumes or gases' with equivalent effect (s.79(1)(c))

- 'any animal kept in such a place or manner as to be prejudicial to health or a nuisance' (s.79(1)(f)).

As with noise nuisance, if you complain to the council about any of these matters it will investigate your complaint but will form its own judgment as to whether intervention is required. In theory, if you are unhappy with a council decision not to act you can bring a court action yourself in the local magistrates' court (s.82).

Before considering taking legal action yourself under the Environmental Protection Act 1990 you should always seek legal advice.

I am being harassed

Harassment can take many forms, ranging from nuisance telephone calls or e-mails to serious intimidation by 'stalkers' or ex-partners. This book is specifically concerned with your housing rights and many of the wider aspects of harassment are beyond its scope. However, as stated at the beginning of this chapter, in serious cases of harassment you should always consider contacting the police.

Before 1997 the law relating to harassment was rather unsatisfactory. In some situations harassment was capable of amounting to a criminal offence (particularly if the victim feared for their own safety). In other situations harassment could amount to a tort (particularly if amounting to intimidation). Further, harassment in the domestic arena, racial and sexual harassment, and harassment by landlords was (and is) dealt with by specific legislation. Harassment by landlords is dealt with in detail in chapter 3. However, neither the criminal nor the civil law seemed to view harassment in itself as necessarily legally wrong in all situations.

Fortunately, in 1997 the Protection from Harassment Act was passed which makes the law a lot easier to understand – and use.

The Protection from Harassment Act 1997

Section 1 of this Act makes it a criminal offence to do anything that the perpetrator knew (or ought to have known) would be likely to amount to harassment of another person. The Act does not define 'harassment' although it does state that there must have been harassment on more than one occasion.

However, it seems clear that the term covers not only threats and explicit intimidation but also 'stalking', offensive and distressing telephone calls, e-mails and letters and methods of debt collection which are humiliating and distressing. The word 'harassment' seems to imply something sustained and intended to annoy or distress.

In a housing context, if your neighbour deliberately intends to annoy or distress you (perhaps because of some other dispute) by loud music or banging on the walls, they may have committed a criminal offence.

The existence of a criminal offence is probably the most important part of the Act, but by s.3 harassment also involves potential civil liability. So you could try to curb your neighbour's future activities by means of an injunction (above) or in extreme cases sue them for damages for psychiatric harm they caused you.

If you feel you are the victim of harassment, complaining to the police is normally the obvious step to take. However, you may also need to take legal advice about whether any civil remedies are also available to you.

I am being accused of nuisance

So far this chapter has covered what you can do if you are the victim of bad behaviour by those around you. If you are the 'accused' much of what has already been said remains relevant, whether this relates to noise, some other nuisance or more general harassment. In such a case three distinct issues need to be considered:

- your vulnerability to being evicted

- the extent to which you are liable for what others living with you do

- anti-social behaviour.

Unreasonable behaviour and eviction

Whatever your legal status in the property where you live (see chapter 2), nuisance or other unreasonable behaviour can make you liable to eviction.

If you have legal protection as an assured or secure tenant the formula is the same, being based on your conduct 'causing or being likely to cause a nuisance or annoyance to a person residing, visiting or otherwise engaging in a lawful activity in the locality'. The wording is a little different in relation to Rent Act statutory tenants (see further on this, chapter 8).

In all cases it is merely a discretionary ground for possession, and re-possession is not automatic, although there is an increasing tendency for outright possession orders to be granted against 'repeat offenders'.

If you are a periodic non-protected tenant or licensee then no reasons for seeking to evict you need to be given (although a court order will usually be required, see chapter 8).

However, in practice 'bad behaviour' on your part will be a very common reason for your landlord seeking to evict you (not least because of the impact your behaviour might be seen to have on co-occupiers or neighbours).

If your non-protected tenancy is a fixed term one it is common to find an 'early termination' or 'break' clause centering on nuisance or other unacceptable behaviour.

If you are at risk of eviction because of (claimed) unreasonable behaviour on your part, seek legal advice, particularly if you otherwise have some security in the property.

Liability for the conduct of others

As a tenant you are generally liable, both in the area of private nuisance, and in relation to eviction, for what your guests and visitors do. Also all joint tenants (see chapter 2) are liable for what other joint tenants do. However, individual tenants or licensees are not intrinsically liable for the misbehaviour of others living in the property who do so under separate licence or tenancy agreements and so are not part of the same household. More difficult is the legal result if your tenancy or licence agreement is written so as to expressly make you liable for what such people do. This is quite common in relation to halls of residence, and quasi-halls run by private landlords in co-operation with universities. The view we take in chapter 7 is that such 'collective responsibility' clauses may be invalid as unfair contract terms. However, this is untested in law and you must take legal advice about it.

Anti-social behaviour

Making excessive noise, or creating other disturbances is clearly anti-social; but as used most commonly at the moment 'anti-social behaviour' normally focuses on criminal activities (particularly drug dealing or violence) which are a problem for the immediate community. We hope you will never be subjected to this kind of accusation; but if you are, there are a number of possible consequences:

- Criminal charges against you.

- The extreme likelihood (discussed above and in chapter 8) that you will face eviction from the house or flat you occupy.

- An injunction being taken out by the council against you, restraining your future activities in the locality.

- An 'anti-social behaviour order' (ASBO) under s.1 of the Crime and Disorder Act 1998. Such orders last for a minimum of two years and could even involve your exclusion from the whole of the area of the relevant council. This would obviously have very serious implications for your ability to continue with your course.

If there is a possibility of any of the above applying to you, seek legal advice immediately.

Students in the community

Universities and colleges are coming under increasing pressure to intervene and mediate or even use disciplinary regulations where students' lifestyles are a cause of friction within the area in which they live.

The issues here are much wider that whether individual students or even student householders are guilty of noise or other anti-social behaviour. In part, any problems are the product of the inevitable tensions caused by rapid environmental change and tolerance to differing lifestyles.

However, rather than face a direct complaint from your neighbour, or even legal action, you may find that your university or college becomes involved. At worst you may find yourself charged under university disciplinary regulations. The view we take in the next chapter in relation to college and university operated accommodation, that such disciplinary sanctions should be balanced and proportionate to the 'offence', obviously applies here as well.

However, it is at least arguable that invoking university disciplinary sanctions about behaviour outside the university, short of criminal conduct, is intrinsically invalid. This is because the university is either acting 'outside its powers' or such a provision amounts to an 'unfair' term.

The use of disciplinary sanctions concerning alleged misbehaviour in the community is becoming more common. Its legality is open to question, although universities themselves would be very likely to invoke their responsibility to the wider community if challenged. However, it is clearly important for students to be sensitive to neighbours who may have different lifestyles to their own.

Case

Adam, Brian, Colin, Darren and Eric rented a terraced house that was owned by an absentee landlord and managed by a letting agency. Complaints about noise were made by the adjoining owner/occupier at the start of the tenancy in August both to the letting agency and the Accommodation Office of the university that the students attended. It was alleged that loud music and foul language emanated from the house on more than occasion in the early hours of the morning, which was particularly distressing as the neighbour had three daughters aged 1, 3 and 5. Although the tenancy agreement was between the letting agency and the group of students, the university was sensitive to concerns about the relationships in popular student areas between students in private accommodation and other local residents.

The university therefore wrote a general letter to the students outlining the complaints and the need to show consideration for neighbours. Subsequent discussions with the students and their parents revealed that only Colin was involved in these particular incidents and that the other tenants were absent.

Further complaints about noise were received from the neighbour in early December, and as well, festive graffiti of an offensive nature had appeared in the windows of the house. An Accommodation Officer from the university called to see the graffiti and spoke to the students about the noise issue. More complaints were received two weeks later from the same neighbour, including a fax sent during a disturbance at 4am. The neighbour could hear loud music and foul language, as well as doors slamming, banging and jumping, which had been preceded by shouting in the street. Complaints from two other residents were also received.

The university now faced a dilemma. It was not a party to the tenancy agreement, but had received detailed complaints about a group of students who did not seem to take heed of informal advice to show more consideration to their neighbours. The letting agency seemed unable or unwilling to take effective action. The university therefore decided to take disciplinary action in accordance with the university regulations which prohibited unreasonable and unruly behaviour.

A formal disciplinary hearing chaired by a senior Accommodation Manager took place with regard to Darren's and Eric's behaviour. The panel heard details of the complaints as well as evidence from Darren and Eric. The panel found that the students had behaved unreasonably, and imposed a penalty in accordance with the university regulations, which consisted of a warning as to future behaviour and a £25 fine. They paid the fine and there were no more complaints about the students' conduct for the rest of the tenancy.

Comment

This case highlights several issues: reluctance of owners or letting agents to deal with complaints and how to deal with repeated behaviour which is causing a nuisance but is possibly not bad enough for the local authority Environmental Health Department to act upon. In this case, the students' behaviour clearly caused distress to the adjoining owner and his family on several occasions. The complaints were specific and detailed, and although it transpired that not all students were involved in all incidents, as a group they were jointly and severally responsible under the terms of the tenancy agreement. There may be some doubt as to whether university regulations should extend to behaviour off university premises and in the wider community. The imposition of a modest penalty appeared to have the desired effect on this particular occasion.

Subjects covered in this chapter include...

Legal status in halls of residence

Head tenancy agreements

The university as both provider of education and landlord

University and college regulations and the law

Disciplinary regulations and student housing

Enforcing rent debts and fines by academic sanctions

Halls of residence

When you consider 'going to university' the image you probably have of your accommodation is of some kind of 'hall of residence' run by the university. Until the 1980s this would have been an accurate image, particularly in the 'old' universities. Even today, in most universities, a majority of first year students live 'in hall' or other university operated accommodation (the alternatives to halls are discussed below). 'Halls', of course, differ considerably in the way they are run. At one extreme (unusual today) is the fully catered hall often complete with linked services such as the cleaning of rooms and even the supply of bed linen (akin to a student 'hotel'). At the other extreme the 'hall' is really a collection of self contained flats. Typically in the latter case each flat would have four to six study bedrooms – individually occupied – and the 'flat sharers' would have a kitchen, bathroom and perhaps communal area in common. Intermediate examples would involve non-catered arrangements but with individual 'study' bedrooms – perhaps with kitchens and bathrooms on each floor.

Although different types of hall might result in you having a different legal status (below) there are important common features, not least the fact that the halls are normally owned and run by the university or college, are provided through some kind of accommodation service as an adjunct to the provision of education and, finally, are occupied exclusively by students at the college or university in question.

Your legal status in halls

In chapter 2 it was stated that many of those living in halls only have a licence rather than a tenancy. The same point is made again in the next chapter. If you do only have a licence your legal rights both during and at the end of the agreement period are limited. However, should it be assumed that all hall occupants are there only as licensees? It is true that most university and college hall agreements use the language of licence rather than tenancy, although they do not necessarily do this consistently. However, as discussed in chapter 2, the courts have established that the wording in an agreement on such matters may not be conclusive. What ultimately counts is the real nature of the legal relationship. Above all, is there exclusive possession in practice? If you occupy a traditional, fully catered hall, it seems likely that you only have a licence because the university or college will retain control of the premises (and not just the common areas) to enable them to provide the catering, cleaning and other services which the agreement provides for. Although there is no case law specifically on halls of residence, cases on retirement home (*Abbeyfields (Harpenden) Society Ltd v. Woods* 1968) lodgers (*Huwyler v. Ruddy* 1995) and hotels (*Luganda v. Service Hotels Ltd* 1969) all point to this conclusion.

On the other hand, if you occupy a 'hall' containing self contained flats, a finding of 'licence' seems much less likely, whatever the agreement states. As a flat sharer you seem to have exclusive possession, either collectively or individually, and there is nothing in the agreement which requires any real control by the university over the day to day functioning of the accommodation. The university might try to argue that it has special responsibilities to remove anyone misbehaving in a hall because of the need to preserve a proper academic atmosphere, and its obligation to the wider student 'community', all of which should lead to the ordinary rules not applying. A not dissimilar argument worked for a council landlord providing a hostel for vulnerable single males in *Westminster City Council v. Clarke* 1992. However, in *Clarke* the vulnerability of the single men, some alcoholics and/or psychologically disturbed, necessitated constant supervision and access. The same can hardly be said for all halls of residence, and 'flat type' halls seem likelier to be viewed as tenancies than licences.

The 'study bedroom with shared communal facilities' arrangement, described above, seems borderline. A lot might depend on how far cooking is allowed in the rooms and how far in other ways they are self contained.

If you do have a tenancy rather than a licence then it will be a non assured (sometimes called 'common law') tenancy. This is because where a landlord is a 'specified educational institution' (which includes all universities and colleges) and the tenant is a student, the tenancy cannot be an assured or assured shorthold tenancy. The relevant law is contained in the Housing Act 1988, Schedule 1, paragraph 8 and the Assured and Protected Tenancies (Lettings to Students) Regulations 1988 (see Appendix E for a full list of specified educational institutions).

What rights does a student have as a non assured tenant?

In general terms, at the end of a tenancy period your rights are not significantly better than if you were a mere licensee.

However, while the tenancy agreement is in force you are protected by the covenant of quiet enjoyment (see chapter 3), you are protected by the repairing covenant in s.11 Landlord and Tenant Act 1985 (see chapter 5) and you do have exclusive possession (see chapter 2). This means that the college or university does not have unrestricted rights to enter your flat (see chapter 3). Moreover, any terms in your tenancy agreement, which conflict with your right to exclusive possession may be invalid. An example could be if the college or university tries to control your right to have overnight guests.

For a more detailed discussion of the rights of non assured tenants see chapters 2 and 8.

The final 'status' issue is whether (assuming you do have a tenancy) this is a sole tenancy or a joint tenancy. This issue is discussed in detail in chapter 2. In most cases, even when a flat is shared, universities create sole rather than joint agreements as first year students in particular will not know each other before taking up residence and it would be inappropriate to group them together. (It may also be because universities think they are licences not tenancies anyway!) In the somewhat unlikely event that you find you have signed a joint occupational agreement with the other flat sharers you should read chapters 2, 4 and 8 to see what the various implications of this are.

Other university accommodation and head tenancies

It was stated in chapter 2 that you should always check the identity of your landlord. When you do you may find that, although you thought the university was your landlord it is, in fact, someone else. Increasingly, universities are entering into arrangements with housing associations and private landlords to provide student accommodation. On occasions, such accommodation may be in halls adjacent to university accommodation. However, in such cases, assuming you do have a tenancy, it will normally be as an assured or assured shorthold tenant rather than as a non assured tenant.

However, in other cases you may be surprised to find that the university is your landlord. It became increasingly common in the 1980s for universities to take over houses and flats from private landlords to let out to students, under what were usually known as head tenancy schemes. In legal terms the university has the main (or 'head') tenancy and then sub-lets to the student occupants (a claim of licence seems very unlikely to succeed here).

As a student your dealings may often be with the owner of the property (or more likely their agent) but in legal terms your landlord is the college or university. As a result, any claims in relation to fitness or disrepair are the responsibility, initially, of the university but, on the other hand, the tenancy is exempted from the usual assured tenancy provisions of the Housing Act 1988 (see chapter 2) because of the fact that the university is your landlord (the Housing Act 1988 Schedule 1 paragraph 8) just as if you were living in hall. Indeed it cannot even be an assured shorthold. If you occupy 'head tenancy' accommodation you are somewhat more likely to do so as a joint tenant than if you occupy a flat 'in hall'. In most respects the rules about joint tenancies are just the same as if you have a private landlord, and are discussed in chapter 2.

The implications of the university's joint role as landlord and provider of education

Universities and colleges, as landlords, are in a distinct position:

- They have clear welfare obligations towards their tenants, and are more likely to be criticised if things go wrong with accommodation.

- However, no other landlord has the apparent power to control, or even discipline their tenants via wider university codes and regulations.

The inter-relationship between the university as your landlord and the university as provider of education to you is a complicated one and, at its widest, beyond the scope of this book. However, given that general university codes and regulations may have a direct bearing on the landlord and tenant relationship between the university and a student tenant it is necessary to examine the area.

Initially, university codes and regulations are looked at in their general legal context.

Then two areas are discussed in detail: disciplinary codes and measures relating to student debt (which can include housing debts).

Finally, the Unfair Terms in Consumer Contract Regulations 1999 are discussed.

University regulations and the law

Traditionally, universities have been reluctant to concede that their relationships with their students are governed by ordinary legal principles. They have always argued that by enrolling at university, a student becomes part of an academic community or institution. The rules of this community are, they argue, like the rules of a private club: perhaps challengeable in extreme cases if they deny such basic legal rights as the right to a fair hearing or exhibiting serious bias or bad faith (see Judicial Review, below) but generally not. In most cases, universities argue, their students only have recourse to internal appeal and 'dispute resolution' procedures. As a last resort, in many of the old universities, there may be a final appeal to the University Visitor (traditionally a figure of high standing and social status – members of the royal family and the Lord Chancellor are popular choices).

The existence of a Visitor does provide for a degree of review and scrutiny external to the university. Check with your student regulations to see if your university has one and, if so, what the procedures are. In general most 'old' universities do have Visitors, and no 'new' ones do.

Even today 'old' universities are very reluctant to admit that the ordinary law has much part to play in their relationships with their students. Two main arguments are used:

- That the university is a chartered corporation and that students, like university staff, are all members of the corporation. 'Arms length' contractual arrangements are, they argue, both legally and practically inappropriate. This is, at root, a variation on the argument already discussed, that everyone is a member of the same 'club'.

- That the existence of the Visitor should normally prevent recourse to the courts.

What is the true legal position?

There may be a distinction between the position of many of the 'old' universities and the position of the 'new' ones ('new' universities are those which have come into being since 1992 – mainly ex-polytechnics). None of the latter have Visitors, nor do they have chartered corporation status. There seems little doubt that the relationship between a 'new' university and its students is a contractual one. The courts may be reluctant to interfere with exercise by the university of pure academic judgment (it is unlikely that you will make such headway in trying to persuade the courts that your assignment should have been given a higher grade!). However, disciplinary codes, descriptions of course and module details, and even matters relating to the award or withholding of qualifications, all seem to be part of the general 'contract of study' between the university and its students. Where the university role as academic provider and provider of accommodation intersect it seems inevitable that the relevant rules and regulations have a contractual basis.

As regards those 'old' universities which are chartered corporations and which do have a Visitor there may be a little more doubt. In the recent case of *Clark v. University of Lincolnshire and Humberside* 2000 the Court of Appeal seemed to say that a contractual claim against an essentially public body, such as a chartered university, was generally inappropriate (the opposite was thought to be true for 'new' universities). This conclusion, however, was not necessary for the decision in the case itself (it is therefore what lawyers call *obiter dicta*) and will not necessarily be followed in future cases.

Nevertheless, if you are considering a contractual claim against an 'old' chartered university you should be prepared for a long drawn out struggle.

Less contentiously it is well established that even a chartered university is bound by public law principles and is potentially subject to its actions being 'judicially reviewed'. If you feel that in applying its rules the university has been guilty of bias against you, has disciplinary rules which prevent impartiality or generally has behaved highly unreasonably, there may be some mileage in a 'public law' challenge.

More debatably, it may be possible to invoke the Human Rights Act 1998 in suitable cases. It seems likely that a university is either a public body or carrying out a public function so as to potentially 'trigger' the Act.

Please bear in mind, however, that taking a case to the high court is a lengthy business even if legal aid is available to assist you, and the extent of the court's power where a Visitor has already become involved is still disputed.

Of course, whatever the legal relationship between a university and its students when it is fulfilling its role as a provider of education, in its role as landlord, the relationship is a contractual one. As in any other tenancy (or licence) agreement there will be various clauses concerning matters such as 'misbehaviour' by the tenants/licensees and non payment of the rent or licence charge. What is unique about the position of the university landlord is that their tenancy/licence agreements (particularly those concerning halls of residence) are normally interlinked with the general disciplinary codes and regulations of the university. Moreover, the university is also in a unique position in that it is able to control non payment of rent and licence fees by treating them as general debts owing to the university with the consequent sanctions attaching to such debts. These two areas are now considered.

Disciplinary regulations and student housing

Almost invariably tenancy and licence agreements used by universities concerning halls of residence contain a clause that the disciplinary rules and procedures of the university apply to actions done by students while in hall. A typical clause might be: 'The university disciplinary rules and procedures apply to this agreement'. Typical 'misbehaviour' covered might be excessive noise, vandalism (including 'pranks' such as letting off fire extinguishers) and harassment of other students (including sexual and racial harassment).

Two different types of result can follow from any such student 'misbehaviour'.

- The tenancy/licence agreement may further provide that any or some specified breach(s) of the disciplinary regulations will lead to the termination of the agreement (either automatically or in specified circumstances).

- The general sanctions in the disciplinary regulations will 'kick in' – typically ranging from fines to suspension from or even expulsion from the university.

From a university perspective it is certainly better to incorporate reference to the disciplinary codes in the tenancy/licence agreement. If this does not happen but instead reliance is placed on the code itself referring back to halls or other university accommodation, there may be issues as to whether the code was given to students too late (this is typically after the hall agreement has been signed). In general terms the law states that for a contractual term to be legally binding it needs either to be in a signed agreement or reasonable notice of it has to be given before the contract is finalised.

As regards termination of the tenancy/licence agreement:

If your agreement is periodic (see chapter 2) then a notice to quit of a minimum four weeks duration is needed to bring it to an end (see chapter 8). No further reasons need to be given by the university since even if it is a tenancy it will be a non assured 'exempt' one because of the Housing Act 1988 Schedule 1 paragraph 8 and the Assured and Protected Tenancies (Letting to Students) Regulations 1998. However, a court order will be needed if you refuse to leave on expiry of the notice to quit.

The need for a court order is not always appreciated by universities. If you are falling foul of a clause requiring you to leave hall or other university owned accommodation, seek legal advice immediately. If your university tries to evict you without a court order, it may be guilty of unlawful eviction (see chapter 3).

If your agreement is for a fixed term (see chapter 2) such as a university term or the academic year there is no need for a notice to quit (see chapter 8) but if the university intends to terminate the agreement before the end of its normal duration there will need to be a 'break' clause in the contract. If the intention is to terminate the agreement because of a breach of disciplinary regulations or other matters such as non-payment of rent, there will need to be express reference to this in the 'break' clause. A court order will, again, be needed if you refuse to leave.

A controversial point concerning fixed term agreements (whether tenancies or licences) is the effect of the Unfair Terms in Consumer Contracts Regulations 1999 (discussed later). No particular reason for seeking possession as such needs to be shown in relation to an 'exempt' university/student tenancy nor as regards a licence. However, if the university attempts to terminate the tenancy/licence before the normal term expires it will only be able to do so if the agreement gives it such a right, and spells out the circumstances where this right can be exercised. Arguably if the reasons given (whether linked to disciplinary codes or not) are 'unfair' they may be unenforceable. This point is, as yet, untested and advice should always be sought concerning it.

As regards general disciplinary sanctions:

The issues raised earlier about the legal status of disciplinary codes applies directly here. On the assumption that the codes have a contractual basis, their enforceability must now be subject to the Unfair Terms in Consumer Contracts Regulations 1999. If, particularly in the case of chartered 'old' universities, their status is more akin to the rules of a club or learned society, they may only be challengeable on a public law basis.

The distinction could be important. If the rules are, effectively, contractual terms they are probably now subject to a general requirement of fairness, whereas if the only legal controls are public law ones in most cases the rules themselves will not be directly challengeable, although their application must be unbiased and operate in an impartial manner.

The following are very common regulations likely to arise when you live in a hall of residence:

- Seeking to impose 'collective responsibility' for damage and vandalism in the hall by way of 'fining' all students in the particular section of the hall irrespective of proof of direct responsibility.

- Imposing fines for being noisy or drunk in hall.

If the basis of the above clauses is contractual (i.e. they form part of some agreement to study between the university and its students) then issues of fairness under the 1999 Regulations might arise. However if their basis is a public law one, challenge under the Regulations would not be possible. Of course, if the disciplinary code is directly incorporated into the hall agreement (which is certainly contractual) then the Regulations should apply in any case.

Case

At 3am University Security received a complaint from Victoria and Melanie in Flat 1 that they were being disturbed frequently by noise from a neighbouring flat and intimidated by Robbie, Giles and Ronan when they went to complain. The security officers entered the flat using a passkey and knocked on the bedroom door several times but there was no reply. It was thought that the music was so loud that the students could not hear. The officers entered the room and one of them introduced himself. He was immediately subjected to verbal abuse. The three occupants of the room refused to identify themselves and stated that they believed they had the right to do what they wanted, as they were paying to live there. The security officers left and reported the matter to the Residences Manager the next day.

A disciplinary hearing was held with Robbie, the official occupant of the room, who was held responsible for the actions of his guests. He was found to be in breach of his tenancy agreement and four of the house rules, which comprised part of the tenancy agreement. A fine of £70 was imposed, along with a final written warning.

Comment

Although this may appear to be a fairly common scenario, it is by no means clear that the university acted within its powers. University staff can only enter students' premises if either the students are licensees or if the letting agreement specifically covers this point. There is also the issue of the appropriateness of fines in the contract: no private landlord would be able to fine a student.

Enforcing rent debts and fines by academic sanctions

It is extremely common for universities to provide in both their disciplinary codes and in their general academic regulations that if any fines or other debts are still owed by a student to the university at the end of an academic year then (as the case may be) the student is not allowed to progress on to the next year of their course or to receive an award certificate. It is normally provided (or at least assumed by the university) that outstanding rent (whether from hall or head tenancy accommodation) is a debt for this purpose. In a few cases the relevant regulations even prohibit graduation. It may also be that some universities still withhold examination results from students until all debts are paid.

A number of issues arise here:

• If the university does still continue to withhold results in these circumstances, this seems to be in breach of the Data Protection Act 1998. Most universities have now accepted this. If yours has not, you should take the matter up with your students' union officer immediately.

• A 'blanket'/automatic denial of 'progression' or graduation, however small the debt, is likely to be a breach of the Unfair Terms in Consumer Contracts Regulations 1999. Such a clause seems excessively one-sided and imbalanced. The regulations are discussed further below.

• Arguably, to threaten such sanctions could be a breach of s.40 Administration of Justice Act 1970 which makes it an offence for a creditor to harass their debtors by excessive or unreasonable demands. Rent or licence charges may, for example, be in arrears because of a dispute over disrepair or the non provision of services (see further chapters 4 and 5). To (in effect) coerce a reluctant student into paying by threatening to withhold their degree is, arguably, harassment. It is certainly the exercise of one-sided power and no other landlord is in a similar position concerning the non payment of rent or licence charges. Please note, however, that this point has not been tested in the courts and further legal advice should always be sought concerning it.

Case

At University A, students are given written information about the university's halls of residence. In that document it says:

'Any outstanding hall rent is treated as a debt to the university and students in debt may be withdrawn from their course or, where appropriate, have their award withheld.'

When students fill in their application form for a place in hall, they sign that they have read and understood this. The tenancy agreement issued makes no reference to this clause.

The university's academic regulations state that:

'Where a student has not yet fulfilled a legitimate requirement of the university, including, *inter alia,* the settlement of any outstanding debt to the university, or to a partner institution at which the student has studied as part of their course scheme at the university, the Academic Registrar may withhold from the student any academic award conferred by the university and s/he shall not be entitled to confirmation of his/her result.'

In the past, the university has withheld defaulting students' results but, in practice, it appears that the university was reluctant to hold back results and awards unless the circumstances were very clear and there was a substantial debt.

It seems that the policy has not been enforced at all for the last couple of years but there has been no publicly stated change of practice or policy.

Comment

It appears that the university has either successfully incorporated the penalty clause into the tenancy agreement or has set up a contract containing the clause. However, the academic regulation is very sweeping in its scope and insufficiently targeted. It is not clear whether the debts referred to relate to the payment of course fees, library fines or the costs of renting college accommodation. As a result, they may be susceptible to challenge.

The Unfair Terms in Consumer Contracts Regulations 1999

Frequent reference has been made already in this chapter to the 1999 Regulations. They replace earlier regulations dating from 1995. In general, the Regulations apply to all terms in consumer contracts, with very few exceptions (none of which would directly apply to universities).

The Regulations apply to all tenancies, public, private and those of educational institutions. They are included in this chapter partly because of the added complexities of the relationships between disciplinary regulations and accommodation agreements and also because there are already some Office of Fair Trading 'rulings' in this area.

An unfair term is any term in a consumer contract which:

• has not been individually negotiated

  and

• contrary to the requirement of good faith, causes a significant imbalance in the parties' rights and obligations arising under the contract

to the detriment of the consumer.

Any unfair term is not binding on a consumer.

The Regulations apply across the European Union and endeavour to create fairer trading conditions for consumers by eliminating any abuse of power by the suppliers of goods and services to them as reflected in the 'fine print' of contracts. Although any consumer affected has the right to take action through the courts, most seek remedies through bodies such as local trading standards departments and the Consumers' Association. Ultimately, most complaints are channelled through the Office of Fair Trading (the address of the OFT is given in chapter 9).

To what extent do the Regulations apply to arrangements between universities and their students?

Universities and colleges contract with their students to supply them with goods and services. These goods and services are normally educational, but can include catering, welfare and (crucially) housing goods and services. Students are the consumers of these goods and services.

Although many universities are reluctant to acknowledge it, the Regulations seem to apply to most such arrangements. Certainly the Office of Fair Trading takes this view, and some universities have already been persuaded to change a number of their rules which the OFT thought were unfair. So far all cases have involved 'new' universities and some 'old' universities may still argue that their arrangements with their students are not contractual ones. It seems doubtful if, in general, the OFT would be sympathetic to this and, in any case, if the rules are included in housing arrangements (tenancies or licences) there seems no doubt that they are contractual in nature. (If you want to read more widely on this, see the OFT website, **www.oft.gov.uk** from which you can download the OFT Guidance on Unfair Terms in Tenancy Agreements.)

What are the implications of the Regulations if they do apply?

In general terms the Regulations make contractual terms unenforceable when they are 'detrimental' to a consumer either because:

- they are excessively one-sided

  or

- the consumer had no real opportunity to become acquainted with them because they were buried in the small print of the contract.

Further, a term may well also be regarded as unfair if it is not clearly written in plain English and is, therefore, difficult to read or understand.

Universities need to be aware that even if terms in their residential agreements or their disciplinary regulations are not excessively one-sided, all too commonly a student is given little or no real notice of them. For example, a hall agreement may be given to a student after they are already in residence and even if it is signed this is amidst a flurry of other documentation. Simpler and more transparent documentation would help combat accusations of unfairness. Comprehensive student charters stressing rights and entitlements as well as obligations would further combat accusations of one-sidedness. Many universities have now acknowledged this and have taken significant steps to make their rules and procedures more transparent and even-handed. However, bad practice can still be found.

In detail, three main areas need to be examined:

- eviction from halls or other university accommodation
- disciplinary sanctions
- student debts.

Eviction

All occupants of university owned or 'head tenancy' accommodation will either be licencees or have non assured 'exempt' tenancies. Therefore if your agreement is a 'periodic' one (see chapter 2) no reason needs to be given to terminate it, and only a four week notice to quit needs to be given, although a court order is required (see chapter 8). Therefore even if a stated reason in the contract is unenforceable as 'unfair' in principle this makes no difference to the university's right to evict if it still wishes to (although it might give them pause for thought).

However, if your agreement is for a fixed period (either an academic term or the whole academic year in most cases) – and this is the norm in halls of residence and very common for other residential agreements – the position may be different. Before a university can evict it needs to 'break' the fixed term agreement before its normal expiry date. An unrestricted right to do so would almost certainly be unfair under the regulations. Even a right to do so for specific reasons may be unfair if either the stated reasons are too wide (for example, a general right to terminate the agreement for 'causing nuisance' or 'excessive noise') or too trivial when compared to the severe sanction of eviction. Of course, serious and specific nuisances or rent arrears may well justify eviction but a clause which has potentially unfair consequences may well be void even if it can equally be used quite fairly.

As stated earlier, the law here is untested but it is the view of the authors that universities should re-examine their fixed term residential agreements to ensure that 'eviction' clauses are as clearly worded, even-handed and proportionate as possible.

Disciplinary sanctions

As discussed above, typical sanctions for 'misbehaviour' in halls range from fines to suspension or expulsion from university. The point about inadequate notice of terms amounting to potential unfairness is particularly significant here. It is doubtful whether a 'blanket' clause such as 'The university's regulations and disciplinary code of conduct apply to this agreement and the student is taken to have read and understood these regulations before signing this agreement' will suffice. At the very least the licence/tenancy agreement itself should spell out in clear and straightforward language what 'misbehaviour' in halls is covered by the disciplinary code and what the potential sanctions are.

As regards the substance of any sanctions imposed, the old saying that the 'punishment should fit the crime' seems relevant. Suspension or even expulsion from the university for (say) a severe case of sexual or racial harassment may be entirely appropriate and 'fair' – as it would be wherever the conduct occurred in the university. Fines for minor damage or vandalism may be another matter. No other landlord/licensor has the power to impose a fine on her/his tenants/licensees – instead other legal steps have to be taken to recover compensation.

Further issues arise concerning 'collective responsibility' clauses, for example holding a whole block or corridor of a hall liable for damage caused in that area irrespective of proof of responsibility. This seems very hard to justify as a fair and balanced clause (certainly if imposed automatically without prior recourse to internal review and mediation).

Finally, 'misbehaviour' in halls may in any case trigger the severe punishment of eviction from hall. Questions may be asked whether it is fair to impose additional sanctions on top of this.

Student debts

Normally a landlord has to pursue outstanding rent claims against a student through the courts. This may be time consuming and irritating but is part of normal legal process. How far is it fair for a university to reserve to itself the sanction of withholding qualifications or blocking progression on to the next year of a course on the basis that rent outstanding is a debt owed to the university and that any debt justifies serious sanctions? The sums involved may be small, or may even be in dispute. This seems a very clear example of (to use the words of Regulation 5 of the 1999 Regulations) a 'significant imbalance in the parties' rights and obligations... to the detriment [of the student]'.

Universities should consider more focused and targeted debt recovery clauses, perhaps reserving the penalty of academic sanctions for serious debts which have been fully investigated and where attempts at internal arbitration or mediation have been made without success.

8

Subjects covered in this chapter include...

What to do if you want to leave

How to give notice

What to do if the landlord wants you out

Who pays the outstanding bills

Recovering your deposit

I want to leave

In virtually all situations, you have to give the landlord notice that you want to leave. How long the period of notice is depends on a number of factors. In practice, how straightforward a process this is will depend substantially on the level of co-operation you get from the landlord. This itself may well turn on the relationship you have already built up with them and the difficulty and cost to the landlord of finding a new tenant. If you have a written agreement, this should provide the basic information you need, though the law may increase your rights in some circumstances.

Agreements for a fixed period

If you have a fixed term agreement, you are bound to continue with it until the end of the agreement period unless there is some provision in the agreement that enables you to leave earlier. While a co-operative landlord can waive this, you cannot force an unco-operative one to accept your early departure. You are contractually bound to pay the rent for the full period you originally signed up to. If you still go ahead and leave, you are likely to lose any deposit paid. You could also be sued for any outstanding balance of rent. However, the landlord is obliged to try to find a new tenant and the balance due would be reduced if the landlord were able to relet. This process is more difficult where the landlord has insisted on the tenant handing over post-dated cheques for the whole period.

Where there is a written agreement for a fixed period, e.g. six months or a year, it will be rare to find a provision that allows the tenant to end it early. However, a longer agreement may contain a break clause.

This will specifically allow either the landlord or the tenant to end the agreement after a prescribed period has run, for example, six months into a one year agreement. It will normally specify how the notice should be given (e.g. in writing and addressed to the landlord) and the notice period. In the absence of such a provision, leaving early is purely a matter of negotiation. Issues that will arise could include the ready availability of a suitable new tenant and the cost of reletting.

Other agreements

Where you do not have a written agreement or are a weekly or monthly tenant, the notice you have to give can vary according to the exact nature of your occupation. The two basic principles are that

- you have to give at least one full rental period's notice, and that

- the notice can only expire at the end of a full rental period.

In most circumstances, a tenant is required by law to give the landlord at least four weeks' notice (s.5(1) Protection From Eviction Act 1977). However, there is nothing to stop the landlord and tenant agreeing on a shorter period. The only exception to the four weeks rule is excluded occupiers. This will mainly affect students who share some accommodation with the landlord or a member of the landlord's family provided the property is their only or principal home (see 'Sharing with resident landlords', page 126, for full details). In this situation, the notice period is calculated solely on the basic principles above.

Example

A tenant who does not share with the landlord and who pays rent on a calendar month basis would have to give a minimum of one month's notice. However, whenever the notice is given, it can only expire at the end of a complete calendar month. Notice given on 16th June would in fact only expire at midnight on 31st July.

How do I give notice?

You should always give notice in writing and keep a copy. This can be done by letter to the landlord and does not require the use of any specific form. Ensure that your letter is dated and that you specify the leaving date. Check the agreement for any specific requirements, for example, an address where the notice should be sent. Although not formally required, it is also sensible to use recorded delivery post to provide evidence that the landlord has received notice should there be a dispute.

Flat sharers: one of us wants to leave

The situation is more complicated where people are sharing accommodation and some want to stay on. It is important to be clear whether the occupants are joint tenants or not (see chapter 2 for details).

(a) The sole tenant leaves

If you have the tenancy, you need to comply with the rules above. The notice period is calculated on the principles explained above. However, you also need to ensure that you give the other occupiers proper notice to leave. They could fall into two alternative categories:

- They are likely to be excluded occupiers where they are sharing the accommodation with you and making payments to you. This means they are at least entitled to some notice that their own arrangements will be ending. Read the section that follows ('The landlord wants me to leave: The private landlord'). Bear in mind that, in relation to them, you are in the role of the private landlord.

- They are your sub-tenants where they have rented a self-contained part of the accommodation from you and you do not share accommodation with them. The law does not allow assured and assured shorthold tenants to sub-let without the landlord's permission. If there has been no permission, the sub-tenants would become trespassers after your tenancy has ended. You should give them appropriate notice to quit.

  If the sub-tenants are there with the permission of the landlord, the sub-tenants would have the same status as the departing tenant. If, for example, the departing tenant was an assured shorthold tenant, the sub-tenants would now become direct assured shorthold tenants of the landlord. Where the landlord knows of the sub-letting and continues to accept rent, this may amount to an implied granting of permission.

Where the remaining occupiers want to take over the property from your landlord after you have left, it might be possible for you to transfer the tenancy to them, though usually only with the landlord's permission. Alternatively, they could negotiate a new letting arrangement directly with the landlord.

(b) A sharer who is not the tenant leaves

If someone else is the tenant and you contribute towards the rent, you are likely to either be a non assured or excluded occupier. If you share some accommodation with the tenant, you will be an excluded occupier (see page 126). In either event, you will have to give a specific notice period depending on any agreement you have with the tenant, or one rental period's notice expiring at the end of a complete rental period. Non assured tenants have to give a minimum of four weeks notice to the tenant.

(c) One of the joint tenants leaves

Where the landlord has rented property to two or more of you, the situation may arise where only one of you wants to leave. Joint tenants are jointly liable for the tenancy. This means that any one of them can be held responsible for the whole of the rent. Simply leaving does not end this responsibility.

The occupiers have five options:

• The remaining joint tenants could simply continue with the existing tenancy, making up the shortfall in rent between them. A leaving occupier who had contributed to a deposit paid to the landlord would want their deposit back. The remaining occupiers could raise this between them with a view to recovering it from the landlord when the whole tenancy ends. Alternatively, the leaving occupier will have to wait until the landlord returns the whole deposit.

• The remaining occupiers find someone to replace the departing joint tenant. It is only possible to bring in a new joint tenant if the landlord agrees. The landlord is not obliged to agree to any new arrangement. Where a joint tenant has left and been replaced to the landlord's knowledge and without their apparent objection, you should seek advice on the situation. It is possible that the landlord has lost their right to object and their behaviour may be taken as an acknowledgment of the new arrangement.

• It may be possible to bring in a new occupier who simply pays a share of the rent to the remaining joint tenants. You need to check your tenancy agreement to see whether this is feasible. Some include clauses that forbid you from 'taking in lodgers'. Breaching this could lead to eviction for everyone.

• The remaining occupiers remove the tenant who is leaving from the agreement and take over the tenancy on their own. They would then have responsibility for for the whole of the accommodation and the rent. In effect this would amount to a new arrangement which would need the agreement of the landlord.

• The departing joint tenant ends their potential liability by bringing the whole tenancy to an end. This would of course result in everyone losing the accommodation. However, where nothing else can be worked out, any joint tenant may be able to end the joint tenancy unilaterally without the agreement of the other joint tenants by giving notice to the landlord. This cannot be done in the middle of a fixed period tenancy but can be done where the tenancy is weekly or monthly or has become one after a fixed period agreement has expired. The notice period is subject to the rules already noted above.

If you are a joint tenant whose rights to remain in a property are threatened in this way you should take legal advice immediately as the courts have recently decided that (at least where you rent from a public body) you may be able to challenge eviction on a human rights basis.

Case

In March, four students agreed to take the tenancy of a flat above a restaurant. In September, a week before the start of the tenancy, one of the students had to drop out as he had failed his re-sit exams, and they sought advice. They were advised to make the landlord aware so he might be more flexible with rent demands, but it was explained that as joint tenants they were responsible for renting the whole property, however valid the reason for one tenant wishing not to move in; and also that they should seek a replacement tenant.

Soon they were back at the Accommodation Office as the landlord, who also owned the restaurant, said he had a chef who needed a room quickly. They were concerned about the compatibility of the group, and liability for Council Tax – as a mixture of students and non-students meant the property would lose its exemption from Council Tax. They were advised that a fourth tenant could not be forced upon them, but they would still be liable for the rent whether or not they accepted the restaurant worker. The fourth tenant may not meet their preferences for a flatmate but might be better than no tenant at all. Eventually, a fourth tenant was found via the Accommodation Office and he moved in two weeks after the start of the tenancy.

The landlord wants me to leave

If a landlord indicates that they want you to leave, two main questions arise:

- Do you have to leave?

- What processes are involved and when will you have to leave?

Whether you have to leave is one of the most complex issues considered in this book. This is because the law protects occupiers according to the kind of landlord and type of residential arrangement they have. Some occupiers have virtually no protection. Other, more fortunate, occupiers can only be evicted against their wishes where they have broken the terms of the agreement and grounds for possession are proved in the county court. In broad terms, people who rent from local authorities and housing associations are likely to have a higher degree of protection than those who rent from private landlords, colleges or universities. However, even the date the tenancy started may be of significance thanks to periodic alterations to the law.

In virtually all cases, letting agreements cannot be ended without the landlord first giving you some written notice. Even after the notice has expired, in many cases the landlord will be committing a criminal offence if they then evict you without having first obtained a possession order from the county court. Where you are being taken to court, you should seek legal advice. You may be eligible for financial help towards the costs of employing a solicitor. See Appendix E for more information.

If you have entered an agreement for a fixed period of time, the landlord cannot usually end it early unless you have broken one or more of your obligations under the agreement, e.g. by not paying the rent or behaving in an anti-social way. However, the landlord will frequently be able to end the letting at the end of the agreement period even where there is no default on your part. Where you are renting on a weekly or monthly basis, the landlord may be able to end the arrangement without any fault on your part simply by giving you the appropriate period of notice to leave.

The college landlord

Accommodation let by universities and colleges can vary through a range of types of hall of residence to individual houses or flats. Protection for the student is determined by the residential arrangement they find themselves in. The letting agreement may describe itself as a licence or as a tenancy. However, the courts have held that the wording in the agreement in itself is not conclusive of the real nature of the relationship between the parties. The issue of exclusive possession is invariably at the core of the legal distinction.

A letting of accommodation in a hall of residence is usually regarded as a genuine licence agreement rather than a tenancy. This is because the student does not have exclusive possession of the room. The university or college retains rights of access to the room and staff may well exercise these rights by entering the room in the student's absence to provide cleaning or other services. The college has overall control of the premises. In these circumstances, the relationship between college and student is governed by the licence. In serious cases, the agreement will allow colleges to ask students to leave after giving a short period of notice.

Even so, not all arrangements involving hall accommodation constitute a licence. Where no services are provided, the accommodation may be in reality more akin to managed flats than the traditional concept of a hall of residence. In these circumstances the occupiers may have a tenancy.

Where the arrangement does involve the student having a tenancy, for example where there is a separate house or flat, the situation depends upon whether the college falls within a list of 'specified educational establishments'. All universities and institutions which provide further or higher education are automatically covered by government regulations along with a number of other specified bodies. (See Appendix A for a full list.) The result is that the arrangement can then at best be regarded as an educational non assured letting as long as kitchen and bathroom facilities are provided. Sharing the use of these facilities with other students does not stop a non assured letting arising.

In order to evict the student, the college must give the student a formal written notice to quit in a prescribed form (see Appendix B). The student is entitled to four weeks' notice and unless they leave voluntarily at that point, a court possession order must be obtained before eviction can take place. However, in deciding whether to grant a possession order, the court will only be concerned that the technical formalities of the notice have been complied with. No specific reasons for wanting to evict, such as not paying rent or causing a nuisance, need to be proved by the college in court to get the order. One disadvantage of staying until a court order is made, though, is that the student will be liable for legal and court costs.

The council landlord

Students who are tenants of local housing authorities (councils) can have a high degree of security. However, your rights can vary according to the exact nature of your particular housing arrangement. In particular, councils can make specific student lettings with much reduced security. In some situations, you might be living in property owned by a local housing authority but managed by your college or a housing association. In these cases, the rules applicable to those landlords will apply.

The basic terms of your relationship with the council will be found in the tenancy agreement. This will explain the circumstances in which you might be asked to leave. However, this is subject to extensive provisions in the 1985 Housing Act (as amended).

While most lettings made by councils constitute secure tenancies, accommodation provided specifically for students can fall outside this category. The council must have notified you in writing before the tenancy starts that this exception to the general rules applies (para. 10, Sch. 1, Housing Act 1985). The notice must indicate that the letting is to enable you to attend a specifically named educational establishment. The tenancy will expire six months after your course finishes. Where you are asked to leave, the terms of the agreement will be significant. They may specify situations where you might be asked to leave. In the absence of specific terms, the council will not need to show any particular reasons for asking you to leave. However, you must be given a written notice to quit. You are entitled to a minimum period of four weeks' notice and, in addition, the notice period can only expire at the end of a complete rental period. If you do not leave at that point, the council must obtain a court possession order against you.

Where the student letting exception does not apply but you have been granted a tenancy within the last year, this may fall within the category of an introductory tenancy. These are probationary tenancies but not all councils use these so check the agreement to establish whether you have one. The agreement should specify the circumstances in which you can be asked to leave within the first year. After serving you with a notice, the council cannot evict you against your will without first obtaining a court possession order. Although the law does not require the council to identify any particular reason for seeking to evict you, the courts have subsequently decided that the council has to give you some reason. However this is a developing area of law and you will need advice. As in most other situations where a court possession order is ultimately made against you, you are likely to have to pay the court costs involved.

The vast majority of people who occupy council property have a secure tenancy. This includes joint tenants who have their names on the tenancy agreement. It may not include a situation where tenants share with other people in hostel type accommodation. If asked to leave, there is a requirement that the council serves you with a notice seeking possession. This is a prescribed form, which must specify the particular basis of the request to leave as well as giving a full explanation of why this particular basis is being relied upon. Subsequently, the council can only end the tenancy by proving this reason in a court. The law here is complex and advice must be sought after receipt of a notice seeking possession.

The private landlord

Landlords other than local housing authorities and housing associations are generally regarded as private landlords. A student who rents a property and then lets out parts to other students is also a private landlord. In some situations, you might be living in a property owned by a private individual or company but managed by your university or college or a housing association. In such cases the rules applicable to the university, college or housing association will apply rather than the rules for private landlords.

With most tenancy agreements made since 28 February 1997, tenants cannot be forced to leave during the tenancy period unless they have broken the terms of the agreement. Once the tenancy period has expired, however, the landlord need not provide any particular reasons for seeking possession. However, your situation can vary considerably depending on your particular arrangements. One of the most significant factors that can reduce your rights is where the landlord lives in the same property as the tenant.

Most students renting from private landlords have assured or assured shorthold tenancies and the rules for the determination of these tenancies are described in detail from the next page onwards. The main exception to these rules in private accommodation is where there is a licence rather than a tenancy, or you have a resident landlord. These exceptions are dealt with first.

Tenants and licensees

The issue of whether you are tenant or licensee (see chapter 2) can be significant. Where you have self-contained accommodation and your landlord has no real control of the premises or a right of access to your accommodation other than to inspect the premises, you are likely to be treated as a tenant. Where you are one of a number of occupiers, you can all be joint tenants where your names appear on the tenancy agreement. Sharing facilities such as a kitchen, bathroom and WC with other occupiers apart from the landlord does not prevent you from being joint tenants.

Typically, arrangements that involve the provision of services such as room cleaning and/or meals and lettings from relatives prevent a tenancy coming into existence. However, it is possible, though not common, to have a tenancy from a relative. This could occur where the terms of the letting are similar to the terms that might exist in a tenancy made between people who are not relatives. Having some self-contained accommodation and paying the going rent for that kind of accommodation would be indicators of a tenancy. A flat or house share, which involves each occupier having a separate and direct agreement with the landlord and where the landlord replaces departing occupiers, may be more indicative of a licence arrangement. This may also be the case where the agreement gives the landlord the right to move you from one room to another, provided this is not purely a notional right.

Genuine licence agreements

Where there is a genuine licence agreement, you will be a non assured occupier. You could even be regarded as a non assured occupier where you live in a self-contained flat in a converted house where the landlord lives in another flat. However, the rule would not apply where the landlord lives in a separate flat in a purpose built block of flats.

As a non assured occupier and in the absence of specific terms in an agreement, the landlord will not need to show any particular reason for asking you to leave. However, you must be given a written notice to quit. You are entitled to a minimum period of four weeks' notice and, in addition, the notice period can only expire at the end of a complete rental period. If you do not leave at that point, the landlord must obtain a court possession order against you.

Sharing with resident landlords

Where you share some facilities with a resident landlord, you are likely to be regarded as an excluded occupier. This scenario applies where you share virtually any accommodation with your landlord or a member of your landlord's family, provided the property is their only or principal home. Only a very restricted area of shared accommodation is ignored here (see s.3A(5)(a) in s.31 Housing Act 1988: accommodation includes neither an area used for storage nor a staircase, passage, corridor or other means of access). There is a fairly extensive definition of 'family' (see s.113 Housing Act 1985).

Excluded occupiers are particularly vulnerable when asked to leave. They are entitled to a notice period where they have an agreement that specifies one, but it is common in these situations merely to have an oral agreement. You will only be entitled to a notice period equivalent to the rental period (e.g. a week or a month) and, in addition, the notice period can only expire at the end of a complete rental period. If you do not leave at that point, the landlord does not actually need a court possession order before evicting you.

Assured and assured shorthold tenancies

Where the landlord is not resident, private tenancy lettings fall into two categories: assured and assured shorthold tenancies.

There are a number of other situations where tenancies cannot be assured or assured shorthold though it is unlikely that they will apply to lettings involving students (Schedule 1, Housing Act 1988). They are:

- Premises with particularly low or high rents. Where the tenancy was granted after 31st March 1990, this covers the situation where the rent is less than £1,000 pa in London (£250 elsewhere) or over £25,000 pa. Where tenancies were granted before 1 April 1990, this is calculated by reference to the old rateable value rather than the rent.

  There may be situations where a student provides part-time assistance to a landlord in return for a much reduced rental payment. An example would be where the student does jobs to support an elderly landlord. The actual rent paid is the significant figure for the purposes of rent limits unless a specific figure has been allocated to the services provided. This would be the case where a higher rent was originally agreed and then reduced to make allowance for the services (*Barnes v. Barrat,* 1970).

- Business premises protected by the Landlord and Tenant Act 1954.

- Licensed premises such as public houses.

- Agricultural land or holdings.

- Holiday lets. Although landlords have used these in the past, they are very rare these days. Despite what some people may think, students are not on holiday.

- Premises rented out by the Crown, local housing authority, new town development corporation, fully mutual housing association or housing action trust tenancies.

Since 28 February 1997, the vast majority of new lettings have been assured shorthold lettings. Unless the letting agreement replaces a previous assured tenancy agreement, they will only be assured lettings where the agreement specifies them as such. Most landlords use written assured shorthold tenancy agreements for a fixed period of time. It is entirely feasible to have an oral assured shorthold tenancy agreement though the problems of interpretation are self-evident.

To evict an assured tenant lawfully, the law requires the landlord to serve a notice on the tenant and, should the tenant refuse to leave, to obtain a court possession order. It only allows landlords to recover possession on certain grounds which are set out in the Housing Act 1988 (see grounds for possession, below). Assured shortholds can be ended either by using a special ground involving two months notice or by using any of the other grounds applicable to all assured tenancies.

Assured shorthold tenancies: two months' notice

The simplest way for a landlord to end an assured shorthold tenancy is to give the tenant a minimum of two months' written notice (s.21, Housing Act 1988). No particular form is required and no particular reason need be cited or proved. However, calculating the exact period of the notice can be complicated:

- If the notice is given at least two months before the fixed period of the agreement expires, it expires on the last day of the agreement.

- If the notice is given later than two months before the end of the fixed period, the expiry date is two months from the date of the notice.

- Where a tenant stays on after the end date given in the tenancy agreement has passed, the tenancy will convert from a fixed period tenancy into a periodic tenancy. In the absence of a new agreement, it is likely to become a weekly or monthly tenancy depending when rent is now payable. In this situation, the landlord must give at least two months' notice and, in addition, the notice can only expire at the end of a complete rental period.

- Where there is no fixed period and the tenancy is periodic, for example, simply a monthly agreement, two months' notice must be given and, additionally, the notice can only expire at the end of a complete rental period.

  (See Appendix C for an example of a notice seeking possession of a property let on an assured shorthold tenancy.)

If the tenant does not leave after the expiry of the notice, the landlord must issue possession proceedings in the county court. The court must grant a possession order provided the landlord proves that it was an assured shorthold tenancy and that the notice was valid. The court can only postpone the operation of a possession order for a maximum of 14 days unless exceptional hardship would result. In exceptional hardship cases, six weeks is the absolute maximum.

Finally, no court can make a possession order that results in the tenant being evicted before six months from the date the tenancy started. This limitation only applies where possession is granted solely on the basis of the landlord giving notice under section 21.

Assured and assured shorthold tenancy: grounds of possession

Where the landlord is not prepared to wait or where you have an assured tenancy, they might alternatively seek to end the tenancy on the basis of one of the grounds of possession set out in the 1988 Housing Act. Many of these grounds relate to default on the tenant's part. Some others depend on the tenant having been given advance notice from the start that the landlord will want the property back in the future for some particular purpose. One example would be where a property is let out by an owner-occupier while she is working abroad and the owner-occupier wants it back on her return.

The notice in all these instances is described as a Notice of Proceedings for Possession and this must be on a specified form (see Appendix B) or in what the law describes as substantially to the same effect. The minimum notice period can vary:

Length of notice	Ground
Immediate notice	14 (tenant causing a nuisance)
Two weeks notice	3, 4 (holiday lets)
	8, 10, 11 (rent arrears)
	12 (other breaches of tenancy agreement)
	13, 15 (wilful damage to the property)
	17 (making a false statement to obtain the tenancy)
Two months notice	1 (owner needs the property to live in again)
	2 (mortgage lender needs to sell)
	5 (property required again for minister of religion)
	6 (demolition or reconstruction)
	7 (inherited tenancies)
	9 (alternative accommodation available)
	16 (accommodation linked to a job)

There is no notice period where the tenant's behaviour is deemed to be anti-social. In most other tenant default cases, the period is two weeks. For other grounds, two months' notice must be given. The notice in all these instances is described as a Notice of Proceedings for Possession. This must be on a specified form (Form No. 3 under Housing Act 1988 section 8 as amended by section 151 of the Housing Act 1996 – see Appendix D).

Even where a fixed period letting has not expired, it may be possible for the landlord to end the agreement and evict you before the period expires. However, the Act restricts the number of grounds on which a court possession order can be obtained i.e. grounds 1, 3 to 7, 9 or 16 may not be used. In practice, this leaves in most grounds that involve some default by the tenant. A court will only make an order on any of the remaining grounds if the terms of the tenancy make provision for it to be brought to an end on any of those grounds. An example from a tenancy agreement is shown below.

Landlord's right of termination

The landlord is entitled to end this tenancy agreement by entering the premises if:

- *any instalment of the rent is not received in full within seven days of the due date (whether or not the landlord formally demands it), or*

- *the tenant fails to comply with any of the tenant's obligations under this agreement, or*

- *the tenant becomes bankrupt or an interim receiver of his property is appointed, or*

- *the tenant (without making arrangements with the landlord or the landlord's agent) leaves the premises vacant or unoccupied.*

The 17 additional grounds for possession, which may be used as the basis for a possession claim, are divided into two main categories: mandatory and discretionary grounds.

Mandatory grounds

Once the landlord has proved that a mandatory ground has been made out, the court is obliged to grant a possession order. The judge must issue an immediate order which takes effect within a maximum of 14 days. In cases of exceptional hardship, this can be extended to an absolute maximum of six weeks.

Discretionary grounds

Where a discretionary ground has been established, the court has discretion whether to grant a possession order or not, or to suspend an order. In making this decision, the court can consider a wide range of factors. It can consider what effect making or refusing a possession order will have in terms of

- the financial gains and losses that the landlord and tenant might make and

- difficulties caused to people living with either party.

It may also take into account issues such as

- how long the tenant has lived in the property

- the landlord's reasons for wanting to obtain possession

- the age and health of the parties and their relatives, and

- whether the situation has affected other occupiers and tenants.

The past behaviour of either landlord or tenant can influence the decision and, in rent arrears cases, the court will also consider the sum involved and the welfare benefits situation.

For more detailed information, see *Defending Possession Proceedings* by J. Luba, N. Madge and D. McConnell, 5th edition, LAG, 2002, pp.203-207.

Where the court decides to make a possession order, it can postpone the date of possession for a period of time, e.g. 28 days. Alternatively, it can suspend the possession order on the basis of the tenant's future conduct. However, the order will take immediate effect if there is a subsequent default by the tenant. In that situation, the landlord is not required to seek a further court order.

Grounds involving rent

There are three grounds for possession involving the payment of rent. The existence of extensive rent arrears constitutes a mandatory ground for possession (ground 8). Extensive arrears are defined as at least eight weeks rent arrears where rent is payable weekly or fortnightly and two months where rent is payable monthly. This level of arrears must exist at the date when the notice of proceedings for possession is served on the tenant and also at the date of any subsequent court hearing. Unfortunately, the reason for arrears is of no relevance to the court. It makes no difference whether you are awaiting a student loan or a cheque from an employer or your parents.

Where there are any arrears when the notice of proceedings for possession was served and when the possession proceedings have begun, this is a discretionary ground for possession (ground 10). Making persistently delayed payment of rent is a separate discretionary ground (ground 11) and whether there are any arrears when the proceedings for possession are begun is decisive.

If discretionary rent grounds are proved, the court can grant an outright possession order or suspend its operation. Suspended possession orders are common in rent arrears cases. However, courts are sometimes less inclined to make suspended orders where arrears are substantial and when the landlord is a private individual. The order will be made subject to the tenant paying the current rent plus an amount off the arrears unless it would cause exceptional hardship to the tenant or would otherwise be unreasonable. If the student breaks the conditions of the suspended possession order by missing one of the payments, the order takes immediate effect. The acceptance of further rent is unlikely to revive the tenancy (see *Burrows v. Brent LBC* 1996). The landlord may then ask the county court bailiff to evict the tenant. This does not require any further court hearings.

Issues that are likely to arise in these cases include:

• Did the tenant have a good record of payment over a period of time?

• Did the arrears arise due to personal circumstances or wilful failure to pay?

• Can the landlord's position be safeguarded by direct payments from the Department of Work and Pensions (where relevant)?

Grounds involving default by the tenant (not involving rent)

There are four discretionary grounds for possession which focus on misbehaviour by tenants. Ground 14 covers the situation where your behaviour constitutes a nuisance or annoyance or where you have been using the accommodation for immoral or illegal purposes.

The nuisance or annoyance can affect not only people who live in the locality but anyone visiting or 'otherwise engaging in a lawful activity' in the locality. While this clearly covers harassment of neighbours, it could also cover inconsiderate and persistent behaviour such as the playing of loud music or the blocking of entrances to the accommodation.

The immoral or illegal activity ground only applies where the tenant has been convicted of an offence that involves the rented accommodation or is committed in the locality. Typically, illegal activities can involve using the accommodation for selling drugs or stolen goods. Convictions involving the possession of small amounts of cannabis are unlikely to trigger evictions. Immoral activities are interpreted as referring to the use of accommodation for prostitution rather than having sex outside marriage.

Causing wilful or negligent damage to the accommodation or ill-treating the furniture that has been provided can fall within grounds 13 and 15. An inventory attached to the tenancy agreement may be of some assistance here, though most do not go into sufficient detail to avoid disputes.

Finally, other breaches of the tenancy agreement not connected with rent can provide the basis for an eviction claim under ground 12. As this is a discretionary ground, not all breaches will lead to a court possession order. Hanging out washing in breach of a covenant not to 'hang on the outside of the premises any flower box flowerpot or similar object or any clothes or other articles' is unlikely to lead to outright eviction but it is conceivable that a suspended order could be made.

Using the accommodation for business activities, however, contrary to the terms of the agreement, would be regarded more seriously and could lead to eviction.

Where a notice is served making allegations of misbehaviour, it is essential to seek legal advice.

Mortgage repossession

It is not uncommon for owner-occupiers who are having difficulty paying their mortgage to let out part or the whole of the property as a way of obtaining extra income to meet the mortgage payments. This means that you can be very vulnerable as a tenant if the landlord subsequently defaults. In some worst case scenarios, lenders have repossessed the property and evicted students without the students having any idea what is going on. Ground 2, nevertheless, provides a mandatory ground for a landlord to evict a tenant where a mortgage lender requires vacant possession of the property to sell it.

Students facing eviction action through mortgage default should ask the university or college accommodation service to negotiate with the mortgage lender. The mortgage lender may be prepared to let the property to the students after repossession, particularly if the housing market makes selling difficult.

Grounds involving prior notice from the landlord

There are four mandatory grounds, which are predicated on the landlord giving the tenant notice before the tenancy started that they would be wanting the accommodation back at some time in future. Even then a court has the power to overlook a failure to give such a notice if it thinks it is fair to do so.

Ground 1 involves two possible scenarios. The first arises where the landlord had at some time occupied the accommodation as his or her only or principal home before the start of the tenancy. The second arises when the property is required as the only or principal home for the landlord and their spouse and the landlord did not buy the property with the tenants already living there.

Ground 3 can be particularly significant to students at universities and colleges in seaside or tourist towns and areas. It allows landlords to let out holiday accommodation over the winter and guarantees repossession when the landlord wants to let the accommodation during the summer to holiday makers. It can be used where the winter let to the student is for a fixed term of not more than eight months, provided the accommodation has been occupied as a holiday letting at some time in the 12 months before the student's tenancy started.

Ground 4 allows universities and colleges to let out halls of residence over the summer, Christmas or Easter vacation periods to tourists and holiday-makers and be sure of getting the property back for the next semester. It can be used where the property is let for a fixed term of not more than 12 months and has been occupied as a holiday letting within the previous 12 months.

Ground 5 applies where the accommodation has been let temporarily but is now required as a residence for a minister of religion.

Suitable alternative accommodation

In some circumstances, a landlord may seek to move a tenant to alternative accommodation. If the tenant refuses to move, the landlord can try to get the tenant evicted from the current accommodation via ground 9. As well as offering a comparable degree of security to the present accommodation, the new accommodation has to be 'reasonably suitable' as regards proximity to work, the rent, and the type and size of the accommodation (Part III, Sch. 2 Housing Act 1988). Apart from the type of tenancy offered, this does not mean it necessarily has to be as suitable (or pleasant) as the current accommodation.

Given that ground 9 is discretionary, the landlord must not only show that the alternative accommodation is suitable but also that it is reasonable for the tenant to be evicted for refusing to accept it.

Where a case on ground 9 succeeds, the alternative accommodation must still be available after the possession order is made.

Substantial building works

Living in accommodation where works are going on is likely to be disruptive for most students. However, ground 6 provides a mandatory ground that can result in a tenant being evicted where the landlord intends to demolish, reconstruct or carry out substantial work on the property. It is a complex ground but ultimately, where the landlord is carrying out substantial work on the property, the student must be willing to allow access. He or she must also be prepared to move into another part of the property to allow the work to be done. Failure to do so could lead to eviction under ground 6. The landlord is not obliged to find you any alternative accommodation following eviction.

Obtaining the tenancy by making a false statement

The landlord can seek possession where it transpires that the tenant made a false statement in order to get the accommodation (ground 17). A student who falsified references from a past landlord or a bank could end up being evicted as a result. However, it must be shown that the statement influenced the granting of the tenancy and that the tenant made the statement knowing it was false or reckless as to its truth.

An inherited tenancy

In very limited circumstances, an assured or assured shorthold tenancy can be passed on after the death of the tenant. However, only a person who is their spouse or co-habitee of the opposite sex qualifies to succeed to the tenancy. Anyone else can be evicted using mandatory ground 7.

Accommodation that comes with a job

If you have accommodation that comes with a job, you could either be regarded as a licensee or a tenant. You will be a licensee if it is reasonably necessary for you to live there in order to be able to perform the job properly. If the accommodation is not reasonably necessary, you could be a tenant. However, if you lose or leave the job, the landlord (and employer) can try to evict you using ground 16.

Registered social landlords (housing associations)

As mentioned in chapter 2, housing associations are independent non-profit making organisations whose function includes the provision of rented accommodation. Most though not all are categorised as registered social landlords (RSLs) through registration with the Housing Corporation. RSLs use the same forms of letting as private landlords. However, very long-standing RSL tenants (whose tenancy started before 15th January 1989) have the same security as secure council tenants, although they have different rent arrangements. However, as well as having their own rules, housing associations are bound to comply with circulars and guidance issued by the Housing Corporation. These aim to ensure that in practice they act in a responsible manner.

Some housing associations provide housing to colleges and the colleges let the accommodation to students. In this situation, the rules about college landlords apply.

However, where you rent directly from an RSL, it will be either on the basis of an assured or assured shorthold tenancy. The notice procedure and grounds for possession are similar to those applicable to the private landlord though you should note the following points.

Rent arrears

In the past, RSLs were constrained in their use of ground 8 (the mandatory extensive arrears ground) but there are now no restrictions on its use and its use is increasing.

Domestic violence

An additional discretionary ground for possession is available to RSLs in some situations involving violence or threats of violence between co-habitees (ground 14A). This can apply where the accommodation is occupied by a married couple or a couple living together as husband and wife. One or both of the partners must be a tenant and one partner must have left because of violence or threats of violence by the other. The threats can be either towards that partner, or towards a member of that partner's family who was living with them immediately before they left. Finally, the court must be satisfied that the partner who has left is unlikely to return.

Things to be sorted out when you leave

Bills

Remember to ensure that you have made the necessary leaving arrangements with service providers such as telephone, electricity and gas companies if you are a direct customer.

If you are a sharer, you should clear your share of any accounts and ensure that the account is transferred out of your name.

Money you have spent on the accommodation

Difficulties can sometimes arise where you have spent money on the accommodation and want to recover this when you leave. Where things are attached to the fabric of a building, they can be regarded as becoming part of the building. As the landlord owns the building, the item becomes the property of the landlord and you would not be allowed to remove it. Tiles put around a kitchen sink or bath would fall into this category. Tiles would be treated as a fixture and would effectively be regarded as a gift to the landlord. You would not entitled to be recompensed unless you had obtained the landlord's agreement to the work and to any financial contribution before any work is started. Doing work without the landlord's approval can lead to disputes. Do bear in mind that what you might regard as an improvement may not be viewed as such by a landlord. The landlord may actually decide to withhold your deposit to pay for restoring things to their original condition.

Recovering your deposit

Disputes about deposits occur frequently when occupiers leave. Landlords can seek to offset any rent owing, unpaid bills or damage caused to the premises against your deposit. Where you think that the deduction is unreasonable or where the landlord refuses to return the deposit at all, you could take action in the small claims court of the county court. Your prospects of success are likely to depend on the evidence you can produce. You should have a receipt from when the deposit was paid. The tenancy agreement should indicate what, if any, deductions the landlord is entitled to take from your deposit. Ideally you will have an inventory listing the contents of the accommodation and its condition, decorative order and cleanliness.

As with any legal action, you need to take into account how much time and energy you are prepared to put into this. You should also bear in mind that you might have to continue the process even after a court judgment where a stubborn landlord still does not return your deposit.

A common practical approach to recovering your deposit is simply to stop paying rent in advance of leaving. Of course, this is likely to antagonise the landlord, as you will be in breach of the letting agreement. However, if the relationship has already soured, it might still be worth considering.

The government is currently funding a pilot scheme (the Tenancy Deposit Scheme) which aims to provide more protection to tenants. The scheme gives the Independent Housing Ombudsman (IHO) the power to decide about the return of deposits. The deposit is put in a special Nationwide Building Society account, overseen by the IHO. Alternatively the landlord can hold the money but must take out an insurance policy that guarantees that the deposit will be repaid to the tenant if the IHO orders.

Subjects covered in this chapter include...

Helpful Internet sites

Accommodation agencies

Gas and electrical installations

How to contact Environmental Health

Useful publications

Other sources of advice and information

Accommodation on the Internet:
sites that offer information about student lettings

This list represents a small selection of what is out there and inclusion in this list does not indicate a recommendation. There are also many companies letting out their own accommodation, which it has not been possible to include. First of all, check the web site of the university or college you will be attending.

www.accommodationforstudents.com (national)

www.letonthenet.com (national)

www.outlet4homes.com (national gay and gay friendly flats, houses and flatshares)

www.homeuk.com (Oxford, London and South Wales)

www.stud-lets.co.uk (Newcastle and Sunderland)

www.net-lettings.co.uk (London)

www.lcos.org.uk (London Student Hostels Directory)

www.studios92.com (short term lets in London)

www.unite-students.co.uk (selection of major cities in England and Scotland)

Accommodation agencies

The Association of Residential Letting Agents (ARLA) is the professional and regulatory body for letting agents. It has rules and guidance that its members undertake to comply with so it might be worth checking whether an agency is a member. Unfortunately many are not. ARLA members should hold any deposit you pay in a designated client's deposit account.

Contact Address:

Maple House
53-55 Woodside Road
Amersham
Bucks
HP6 6AA

Tel: 0845 345 5752

Web site: **www.arla.co.uk**

Advice and solicitors

Law centres, Shelter Housing Aid Centres, advice centres, and Citizens' Advice Bureaux can usually help with housing problems. The Legal Services Commission has granted legal aid franchises to solicitors and to advice centres for housing cases. The best way to find local advice, help and your nearest solicitor with a legal aid franchise is via the Government's Community Legal Service web site at **www.justask.org.uk**

You can also find a solicitor via the Law Society's web site **www.solicitors-online.com** though you cannot search for housing specialists.

Housing advice is also available online via Shelter's web site at **www.Shelternet.org.uk**

Court service

The court service web site **www.courtservice.gov.uk** provides useful information about how the courts work. Above all, however, it is the place to begin if you want to find out about pursuing a small claim in the county court. You can even begin a small claim on-line via the web site.

Commission for Local Administration (Local Government Ombudsman)

For complaints about maladministration of housing benefit or council tax benefit.

Advice line: 0845 602 1983
Web site: **www.lgo.org.uk**

Commission for Racial Equality (CRE)

Elliot House, 10-12 Allington Street, London SW1E 5EH

Tel: 020 7828 7022

Web site: **www.cre.gov.uk**

Deposits

You can find more information about the Tenants Deposit Scheme from the Independent Housing Ombudsman, Norman House, 105-109 Strand, London WC2R 0AA

Tel: 020 7379 1754 or 0845 601 1200
Web site: **www.ihos.org.uk/tds/about.htm**

Disability Rights Commission (DRC)

222 Grays Inn Road, London WC1X

Tel: 08457 622633
Web site: **www.drc-gb.org**

Electricity

National Inspection Council for Electrical Installation Contracting (NICEIC): **www.niceic.org.uk**

Electrical Contractors Association (ECA): **www.eca.co.uk**

Environmental Health Officers

Environmental Health Officers (EHOs) can help if your home is in a bad state of repair and particularly if there is a health risk involved.

Contact them at your local council. They are usually found in a separate Environmental Health Department but may be found in a consumer protection or similar department. Make it clear that you want to talk to an EHO.

Furnishings and furniture

A Guide to the Furniture and Furnishings (Fire) (Safety) Regulations. Download from **www.dti.gov.uk/access/furniture/intro.htm** or free booklet available from DTI Publications Order Line, Admail 528, London SW1W 8YT, telephone 0870 1502 500.

Gas safety

Gas Safety Advice Line: 0800 300 363.

Gas appliances – get them checked, keep them safe.
The leaflet is available free from the Health and Safety Executive,
PO Box 1999, Sudbury, Suffolk CO10 6FS

Tel: 01787 881165
Fax: 01787 313995.

Independent Housing Ombudsman

3rd floor, Norman House, 105-109 The Strand, London WC2R OAA

Tel: 020 7836 3630
Web site: **www.ihos.org.uk**

Lesbian and Gay Switchboard

Tel: 020 7837 7324

Refugee Council

3 Bondway, London SW8 1SJ

Tel: 020 7820 3085
Web site: **www.refugeecouncil.org.uk**

Shelter

Shelter has a 24-hour emergency housing helpline called Shelterline
(freephone 0808 800 4444) and a network of over 50 housing aid
centres (HACs) and projects around the country. For the address of your
nearest HAC or project call 020 7505 2000.

Student Union

Your university or college Student Union may have a sabbatical officer
who specialises in housing advice, or a Welfare Officer who can provide
advice on a wide range of issues including student accommodation.

Tenants Deposit Scheme

See 'Deposits' on page 143.

Tenancy agreements

Unfair tenancy terms: don't get caught out.
A useful leaflet about unfair tenancy terms can be ordered from the
Office of Fair Trading, Fleetbank House, 2-6 Salisbury Square,
London EC4Y 8JX.

Tel: 0870 6060321
Fax: 020 7211 8800.

You can also download it in pdf format from
www.oft.gov.uk/News/Publications/leaflet+ordering.htm
It is not named there but is *oft381.pdf*

Tenancy Relations Officers

Tenancy Relations Officers (TROs) can assist tenants who are being
harassed or have been illegally evicted by their landlord. Some also
deal with accommodation agencies that make illegal charges.

Sometimes they are to be found in council housing departments and
sometimes in consumer protection departments. So you need to make
it clear to the person you speak to exactly what problem you have.
According to a 1995 survey, about 30% of local authorities employ
tenancy relations officers. The figure rises to over 50% for metropolitan
authorities and 80% for London boroughs.

Other local authority officers also carry out tenancy relations work.
If your local authority does not have a TRO ask your local authority
Housing Department who is responsible for tenancy relations.

Useful publications which are regularly updated

Manual of Housing Law
Andrew Arden QC and Caroline Hunter
Published 1996
Sweet & Maxwell
ISBN: 0 421553 901

Guide to Housing Benefit and Council Tax Benefit 2002-03
John Zebedee and Martin Ward
Published 2002
Shelter
ISBN: 1 903208 319

Council Tax Handbook
Published 2002
CPAG
ISBN: 1 901698 483

Fuel Rights Handbook
N. Nicol and C. Bartholomew
Published 2002
CPAG
ISBN: 1 901698 38

Housing Rights Guide
Geoffrey Randall
Published 2002
Shelter
ISBN: 1 870767 926

Series of Shelter Guides:
Homeless? Read this
Finding a place to live
Housing Association Tenants
Private Tenancies

Women's Aid Federation

National helpline: 0345 023468
Web site: **www.womensaid.org.uk**

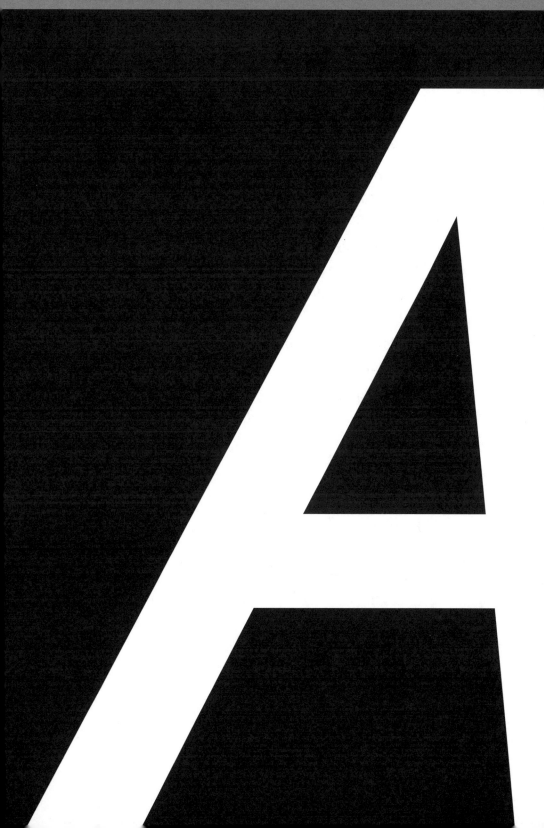

Subjects covered in this section...

Appendix A:
Specified educational institutions whose lettings to students can be neither assured nor assured shorthold

Appendix B:
Information that must be included in a notice to quit (non-assured lettings)

Appendix C:
Notice seeking possession of a property let on an assured shorthold tenancy

Appendix D:
Notice seeking possession of a property let on an assured tenancy

Appendix E:
Public help for defending possession cases

Appendix A:

Specified educational institutions whose lettings to students can be neither assured nor assured shorthold

The specified educational institutions are:

- any university or university college and any constituent college, school or hall or other institution of a university (or their governing bodies)

- any other institution which provides further education or higher education or both and which is publicly funded;

- any body, other than a local education authority, providing any such educational institution;

- any registered housing association, and

- the following specifically listed bodies:

AFSIL Limited

Campus Accommodation Ltd
(added by Statutory Instrument 1999 No.1803)

The David Game Tutorial College, London

Derbyshire Student Residences Limited

Friendship Housing

Hull Student Welfare Association

International Lutheran Student Centre

International Students Club (Church of England) Limited

International Students' Club (Lee Abbey) Limited

International Students Housing Society

Oxford Brookes Housing Association Limited

Oxford Overseas Student Housing Association Limited

St Brigid's House Limited

St Thomas More Housing Society Limited

SOAS Homes Limited
(added by Statutory Instrument 2000 No. 2706)

International Students House
The London Goodenough Trust for Overseas Graduates

The House of St. Gregory and St. Macrina Oxford Limited

The London Mission (West London)
Circuit Meeting of the Methodist Church

The London School of Economics Housing Association

The Royal London Hospital Special Trustees

The Universities of Brighton and Sussex Catholic
Chaplaincy Association

The Victoria League for Commonwealth Friendship

University of Leicester Students' Union

Wandsworth Students Housing Association Limited

Willowbrook Properties Ltd
(added by Statutory Instrument 1999 No. 2268)

York Housing Association Limited

See The Assured and Protected Tenancies (Lettings to Students) Regulations 1998 (Statutory Instrument 1998 No. 1967) and amendments.

Appendix B:

Information that must be included in a notice to quit

The Notices to Quit etc (Prescribed Information) Regulations 1988

Prescribed information

1 If the tenant or licensee does not leave the dwelling, the landlord or licensor must get an order for possession from the court before the tenant or licensee can lawfully be evicted. The landlord or licensor cannot apply for such an order before the notice to quit or notice to determine has run out.

2 A tenant or licensee who does not know if he has any right to remain in possession after a notice to quit or a notice to determine runs out can obtain advice from a solicitor. Help with all or part of the cost of legal advice and assistance may be available under the Legal Aid Scheme. He should also be able to obtain information from a Citizens' Advice Bureau, a Housing Aid Centre or a rent officer.

Appendix C:

Notice seeking possession of a property let on an assured shorthold tenancy
(note that no specific form is required)

Assured Shorthold Tenancy:
Notice requiring Possession

To *[tenant's name]*
of *[tenant's address]*

From *[landlord's name]*
of *[landlord's address]*

I give you notice that I require possession of the premises you are renting at *[address of premises]* on *[date at expiry of correct notice period]*

Dated *[date served]*

Landlord's signature ....

[Landlord's name]
[Landlord's address]

Appendix D:

Notice seeking possession of a property let on an assured tenancy

Notice seeking Form No. 3

Housing Act 1988 section 8
as amended by section 151 of the Housing Act 1996

Notice seeking possession of a property let on an Assured Tenancy or an Assured Agricultural Occupancy

- Please write clearly in black ink.

- Please tick boxes where appropriate and cross out text marked with an asterisk (*) that does not apply.

- This form should be used where possession of accommodation let under an assured tenancy, an assured agricultural occupancy or an assured shorthold tenancy is sought on one of the grounds in Schedule 2 to the Housing Act 1988.

- Do not use this form if possession is sought on the 'shorthold' ground under section 21 of the Housing Act 1988 from an assured shorthold tenant where the fixed term has come to an end or, for assured shorthold tenancies with no fixed term which started on or after 28th February 1997, after six months has elapsed. There is no prescribed form for these cases, but you must give notice in writing.

1. To:

   Name(s) of tenant(s)/licensee(s)*

2. Your landlord/licensor intends to apply to the court for an order requiring you to give up possession of:

   Address of premises

3. Your landlord/licensor* intends to seek possession on grounds(s) [3] in Schedule 2 to the Housing Act 1988, as amended by the Housing Act 1996, which read(s):

Give the full text (as set out in the Housing Act 1988 as amended by the Housing Act 1996) of each ground which is being relied on. Continue on a separate sheet if necessary.

4. Give a full explanation of why each ground is being relied on:

Continue on a separate sheet if necessary

Notes on the grounds for possession

- If the court is satisfied that any of grounds 1 to 8 is established, it must make an order (but see below in respect of fixed term tenancies).

- Before the court will grant an order on any of grounds 9 to 17, it must be satisfied that it is reasonable to require you to leave. This means that, if one of these grounds is set out in section 3, you will be able to suggest to the court that it is not reasonable that you should have to leave, even if you accept that the ground applies.

- The court will not make an order under grounds 1, 3 to 7, 9 or 16, to take effect during the fixed term of the tenancy (if there is one) and it will only make an order during the fixed term on grounds 2, 8,10 to 15 or 17 if the terms of the tenancy make provision for it to be brought to an end on any of these grounds.

- Where the court makes an order for possession solely on ground 6 or 9, the landlord must pay your reasonable removal expenses.

5. The court proceedings will not begin until after:

Give the earliest date on which court proceedings can be brought

Where the landlord is seeking possession on grounds 1, 2, 5 to 7, 9 or 16, court proceedings cannot begin earlier than two months from the date this notice is served on you (even where one of the grounds 3, 4, 8, 10 to 13, 14A, 15 or 17 is specified) and not before the date on which the tenancy (had it not been assured) could have been brought to an end by a notice to quit served at the same time as this notice.

Where the landlord is seeking possession on grounds 3, 4, 8, 10 to 13, 14A, 15 or 17, court proceedings cannot begin earlier than two weeks from the date this notice is served (unless one of 1, 2, 5 to 7, 9 or 16 grounds is also specified in which case they cannot begin earlier than two months from the date this notice is served).

Where the landlord is seeking possession on ground 14 (with or without other grounds), court proceedings cannot begin before the date this notice is served.

Where the landlord is seeking possession on ground 14A, court proceedings cannot begin unless the landlord has served, or has taken all reasonable steps to serve, a copy of this notice on the partner who has left the property.

After the date shown in section 5, court proceedings may be begun at once but not later than 12 months from the date on which this notice is served. After this time the notice will lapse and a new notice must be served before possession can be sought.

6. Name and address of landlord(s)/licensor(s)*

To be signed and dated by the landlord or licensor or his agent (someone acting for him). If there are joint landlords each landlord or the agent must sign unless one signs on behalf of the rest with their agreement.

Signed

Date

Please specify whether

☐ landlord
☐ licensor
☐ joint landlords
☐ landlord's agent

Name(s)

(BLOCK CAPITALS)

Address

Telephone

Daytime

Evening

What to do if this notice is served on you

- This notice is the first step requiring you to give up possession of your home. You should read it very carefully.

- Your landlord cannot make you leave your home without an order for possession issued by a court. By issuing this notice your landlord is informing you that he intends to seek such an order. If you are willing to give up possession without a court order, you should tell the person who signed this notice as soon as possible and say when you are prepared to leave.

- Whichever grounds are set out in section 3 of this form, the court may allow any of the other grounds to be added at a later date. If this is done, you will be told about it so you can discuss the additional grounds at the court hearing as well as the grounds set out in section 3.

- If you need advice about this notice, and what you should do about it, take it immediately to a citizens' advice bureau, a housing advice centre, a law centre or a solicitor.

Appendix E:

Public help for defending possession cases

Public Funding from the Legal Services Commission (LSC) is frequently available for funding the defence of possession proceedings. There are two schemes.

Public funding certificates

If a public funding certificate is obtained, it will pay the costs of employing a solicitor and of other necessary expenses (barrister's fees, survey fees, etc). However, to be eligible for assistance, you must come within the financial limits and have a substantive defence, i.e. pass the means test and the merit test.

A solicitor who has a franchise in the housing category can grant him/herself a public funding emergency certificate if they are instructed shortly before the hearing. This will normally be limited to steps up to and including the first hearing. If instructed in good time, an application can be made to the LSC for a public funding certificate.

The means test

Your financial means must be low enough to enable you to get free assistance or assistance with a contribution. A person on Income Support or Income Based JSA will be 'passported' and will get free legal assistance.

If your income is very low, you will get free assistance. A person who earns less than £24,000 pa may be eligible for a public funding certificate. If you have a modest income, you may be eligible for assistance subject to paying a contribution. A person's savings and capital can also be taken into account. The LSC publishes guidance, which must be followed to calculate whether a person is eligible.

The merit test

There must be a real prospect of defeating the claim rather than merely an attempt to delay the making of a possession order. The test considers whether the defence or claim to be funded is likely to succeed. If the merits are 'very good' (80% plus) or 'good' (60-80%) then the merit test will be satisfied. If the merits are 'borderline' (50-60%) the merit test may still be met in possession cases (subject to compliance with guidance). If the merits are 'poor' (less than 50%) then only in exceptional circumstances will the merit test be met.

Legal help and help at court

This scheme is available to people who pass the means test. It is useful in two circumstances.

Firstly, where instructions are given in good time and there is a substantive defence, the solicitor will make an application for a public funding certificate. It will take the LSC two to three weeks to process the application. In the meantime, the solicitor can carry out work and incur disbursements (expenses) of up to £500 under the Legal Help scheme in steps up to but not including engaging in the litigation. This would cover, for example, correspondence with the claimant or commissioning a survey report. An application can be made to the LSC to increase the upper cost limit of £500.

Secondly, a solicitor can attend court for the defendant under this scheme where there is only a technical defence or where the only issue is whether the defendant should have an outright order suspended for six weeks because of exceptional hardship.

The Legal Help scheme is also commonly available to obtain advice and assistance about sorting out housing benefit problems, which are causing, or adding to, rent arrears.

Index

F

fire precautions 67

fitness for human habitation 76

fixed term agreement 117

fixed term tenancy 16

flat sharers 118

flat-mates 88

forfeiture clauses 37

furnishings 67, 143

G

gas 144

Gas Safety Regulations 1998 66

grounds for possession 53, 92, 128, 130, 131

guests 92, 100

H

halls of residence 4, 14, 20, 60, 88, 99, 122, 133

harassment 33, 36, 39, 83, 90, 91, 132

head tenancy 4, 21, 88, 101

help at court 158

holiday accommodation 133

house in multiple occupation 67, 74, 78

housing association 23, 135

Housing Benefit 43, 44, 60

Human Rights Act 1998 104

I

illegal activities 132

improvement 136

internet 6

introductory tenancy 124

inventory 49

J

joint tenancy 17, 18, 54, 88, 92, 101, 120

K

keys 36, 37

L

legal advice 122, 158

length of agreement 7

licence 12, 20, 28, 36, 44, 71, 99, 122, 123, 125, 126

lodger 5, 13, 24, 120

M

means of escape 67

mesne profits 44

minors 16

misbehaviour 21

mortgage repossession 133

T

tenancy agreement 29, 145

tenancy deposit scheme 49, 137

tenancy/licence distinction 13, 122, 125

Tenancy Relations Officer 37, 145

tenant's obligations 68

termination 54, 105

U

unfair tenancy terms 145

Unfair Terms in Consumer Contracts
    Regulations 1999 14, 20, 106, 108,
    110

unfit for human habitation 74

university regulations 102

University Visitor 102

unlawful eviction 36, 39

V

visitors 92

W

wear and tear 49

withholding rent 54

written statement of basic tenancy
    terms 26